POINT PARK ID
Required for check-out

D1247254

TELEVISION WRITING
From Concept to Contract

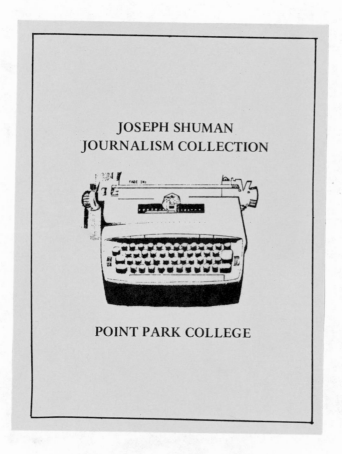

TELEVISION
WRITING

From Concept to Contract

by Richard A. Blum

COMMUNICATION ARTS BOOKS

HASTINGS HOUSE · PUBLISHERS

New York 10016

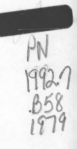

For Barbara, Jason, and Jennifer

Library of Congress Cataloging in Publication Data

Blum, Richard A
  Television writing.

  (Communication arts books)
  Bibliography: p.
  Includes index.
  1. Television authorship. I. Title.
PN1992.7.B58 1980   808'.025   79-23248
ISBN 0-8038-7208-9
ISBN 0-8038-7209-7 pbk.

Published simultaneously in Canada by Copp Clark, Ltd., Toronto

Designed by Al Lichtenberg
Printed in the United States of America

Contents

Acknowledgments

There are many people who have contributed to this book, and I'd like to express my appreciation to them all. Dozens of my colleagues in the industry and academic world have shared their ideas, suggestions, and enthusiasm. My friend, Frank Tavares has been particularly generous in that regard. For all the direct and indirect feedback, my thanks.

I would also like to thank my students who served as the impetus for this book. The questions asked, issues discussed, projects written, and experiences shared, helped codify the concerns of talented new writers. I hope this book now addresses some of those concerns in a manageable and practical fashion.

There could be no book without support from those on the homefront. I'm grateful to my wife, Barbara, whose intelligent critiques helped move this manuscript from the drawing boards to final draft. My children, Jason and Jennifer, were most understanding of the partially closed door of my study. I appreciate their patience. I want to thank Eve Blum for her many valuable suggestions and insights. I also received sound advice and feedback from Irving and Ida Feirstein.

On the editorial side, I'd like to express my appreciation to Russell F. Neale, Publisher, *Communication Arts Books,* for his dependable support and guidance throughout the various stages of this work. I also want to thank Jim Moore, his assistant, for such easy accessibility whenever questions about the manuscript came up.

• • •

For permission to reprint excerpted materials, I would like to thank my writing partners and the following copyright owners:

"Compute-a-Quiz," co-written with Larry Frank, Pres., Laurence Frank & Co., 1801 Ave. of the Stars, Century City, Calif. 90067. All rights reserved.

"Death's Head," Episode #1 ("Circle of Fear" series) written by Rick Blum, reprinted with permission of Columbia Pictures Industries, Inc. All rights reserved.

"Disappearing Act," co-written with Robert Lovenheim, River City Productions, Los Angeles, Calif. All rights reserved.

"Glues Company," Episode #2 ("The New Little Rascals" series) written by Dan Wilcox. © copyright 1977 TAT Communications Co. All rights reserved.

"Intercept," co-written with Hank Hamilton. All rights reserved.

"Masks & Faces," co-written with Hart Sprager, Pres., Spectrum IV Productions, Austin, Texas.

"Schools With Screenwriting Courses," adapted from *The American Film Institute Guide to College Courses in Film and Television,* Sixth Edition, by permission of the American Film Institute, John F. Kennedy Center for Performing Arts, Washington, D.C.

"The Watchmaker," adapted for TV by Rick Blum, based on the novel, *A Teaspoon of Honey* (Aurora Publishers, Inc.) by Bert Kruger Smith. Reprinted with permission of the author, and Fred Miller, producer. © The Honey Production Company. All rights reserved.

"Wind Chill Factor," co-written with Dan Wilcox. All rights reserved.

"Writers Guild of America, Theatrical & Television Basic Agreement," excerpts reprinted with permission of Writers Guild of America, West.

"Ziggy's Gang," co-created with Rick Kaiser for Universal Studios. All rights reserved.

Introduction

If you're an aspiring television writer, you've probably tried your hand at writing some episodes for the latest series on TV. You may have sent one of the scripts to a series producer and waited anxiously for some career-changing response. That script was most likely returned, unopened, with a form letter attached: "Sorry, we don't read unsolicited material." Or, if you were lucky, a personal note: "We already have something similar in work." Or any variant thereof. Sound familiar?

Then you've discovered the reality of script submission—the producer of a current series is the *wrong* person to send an original script, and the unsolicited TV episode is the *least* likely to be sold. A series producer is concerned about Nielsen ratings, deadline pressures, and network paranoia. He or she has no time to nurture an unsold writer or to develop an unassigned script. Moreover, a series producer usually assigns scripts to "heavyweights" early in the development season. These are writers who have worked successfully in the genre, who are adaptive in story conferences, who are fast and reliable in meeting script deadlines.

Other variables come into play as well. While you've written an hilarious episode taking place in a country school house, the network has already decreed that the series must be less slapstick, more urban, more relevant, more romantic, etc. There may also be shifts in character emphasis with less stress on the lead, and greater emphasis on two minor characters in the series. There is no way for you, sitting at home with your typewriter, to know the gist of story conferences, phone calls, and daily exchanges of memos. Once you've seen the format changes on the screen, new series modifications are already being discussed and implemented at the studio.

There is another reason why speculative writing for an on-going series is a futile route for the beginner. It's virtually impossible to know the premises of all stories in development at the studio. Given the range of series episodes, it's not unlikely that your story idea comes pretty close to another that was aired, discussed with other writers, or turned down in some other form. And that raises another reality. Producers are concerned that a freelancer may sue for plagiarism if a show looks similar to the unsolicited script. That's another reason "unsolicited" material is returned to the author without being read.

If a television script for an on-going series is the wrong way to break in, how does a writer show his or her potential for the medium? The same way professional writers do—by creating *original* shows for television. Specifically, this means developing original TV series presentations, or developing treatments and scripts for pilots, movies-of-the-week, or mini-series. The original project is unfettered by the dictates of another author's characters, formula situations, or pre-established conflicts that have been aired for two years. When you create a new television series or long-form drama, you're developing ideas directly for the medium. You're competing in the mainstream of new ideas. A well written television project shows you can effectively bring to life your own characters and formats, dramatic situations, and visual action. It shows your knowledge of the marketplace, as well as your grasp on writing technique. And that puts you in an enviable position compared to the beginning writer who is still turning out speculative scripts for a series that has just been cancelled.

There is something very gratifying about developing new television projects. Perhaps it relates to the eternal fantasy of *doing* something about television. Just think of the average American TV viewer, staring at the set for almost seven hours a day. He or she is bombarded with drama and comedy from the same network mold, with only slight variations from season to season. In a very real way, this book is about how *you* can help change that picture, and upgrade the programming fare watched by millions of Americans every night. It's a worthy fantasy to pursue.

● ● ●

This book focuses on the techniques and formats used by professionals to sell their ideas in the most polished form. Part One deals exclusively with TV program proposals and series presentations. Although this form of writing is one of the most consistent moneymakers, the series format is not generally made available to newcomers. There is no major conspiracy involved and I doubt if writers are protecting themselves from outside competition. Rather, formats are simply never published and rarely handed down. This book, I hope, will offset that problem by providing specific examples, ideas, and guidelines for writing new dramatic and comedy series for networks and studios, as well as variety specials and quiz programs.

Although we will concentrate on the network television marketplace, it is not the only avenue for submission of new ideas. For that reason, Part One also covers the marketplace needs and format requirements for non-commercial television (specifically public TV and federal agencies). The opportunities for funding new projects in these areas are very real, and the possibilities for script writing grants are substantial.

Part Two discusses the theory and practice of writing pilot stories and movies-of-the-week treatments. It deals with the problems of story and character development for dramatic shows, and details the most effective devices for developing plots and story outlines. Moreover, it shows how *Method* acting techniques can be used for developing characters in the story and script, and how dialogue problems can be identified and corrected in the script phase of writing.

Part Three concentrates on the specific formats involved in writing scripts for TV film and videotape. That's because no producer, program executive, or agent will pick up a script unless it's in the proper form. All worthy projects won't be produced—in fact, most scripts won't even be read—but if the project is well written in concept, style, and form, it stands a much better chance of being evaluated. Technique and form are essential for writers who seriously intend to enter the mainstream of the profession. Just as an actor learns basic techniques to create effectively, so the television writer learns every technique of writing, from the germination of an idea to the revision of a final draft. If the stress on form seems a bit dogmatic at times, please remember that competition is incredibly stiff and a professional-looking script can help you past that first major hurdle—getting the project read.

Part Four deals with the pragmatics of marketing the property—how, when, where, and to whom it should go. The odds against selling a new project are staggering, but without a knowledge of the marketplace there's no glimmer of hope for success. This section answers key questions every writer should know: How do you get a producer to read the project? How and where do you submit it? What happens if a producer is interested? What contractual arrangements can be expected? How do you get an agent?

The writer who stands the best chance of making it is the one with industry awareness and contacts, coupled with talent, technique, and indomitable perseverance. If you're willing to confront incredible odds with highly imaginative program concepts, perseverance might eventually pay off. The industry consumes thousands of stories and scripts every television season. It requires a horde of able writers to keep those home lights burning. This book can provide you with certain writing techniques—from form to marketing—but only you can provide the essential ingredients of talent and creativity. Once you know the form, the demonstration of imagination and style is up to you. Why not put them to work and see what happens?

PART ONE

PROGRAM PROPOSALS

AND SERIES PRESENTATIONS

2

Commercial TV Presentations: Drama and Comedy

The Networks and Program Development

A program development executive receives hundreds of submissions each week—sometimes over the phone, sometimes in skeletal proposals, sometimes in fully detailed presentations. He or she is responsible for bringing new ideas into the network. Once the show actually gets on the air, another department takes over—current programming or primetime programming. That department is concerned with time slots, competition, demographic appeal, lead-in and lead-out programs, and other factors that will affect the ratings performance of a series on the air. The goal is always the same: to reach the largest number of television homes in the country.

Job security in programming is about as secure as the changing decimals on the overnight Nielsen ratings. So, understandably, some executives view innovative program concepts as a threat rather than a challenge. Jobs are literally dependent upon ideas that are greeted with enthusiasm by superiors, advertisers, and the whimsical public.

If an executive pushes for an innovative show and it fails, the Want Ads will soon be top priority reading. If the show is based on a proven formula (*i.e.* modeled after a highly successful show), the personal risk is somewhat lessened. The executive can always point to the unpredictable tastes of the viewing public.

Does this mean you have to create the same kind of formula programs you see every night? In one sense, yes; in another sense, no. Let me explain. Television is an imitative medium. It thrives on successes, and spits out a slew of carbon copies, spin-offs, and character duplicates in an effort to reach the same wide audiences as the original. We've all experienced the glut of westerns, medical shows, police shows, and so on. If television is out for the greatest possible audience, why doesn't it break away from the trends rather than imitate them? A theory of *L.O.P.* was proposed by former network executive Paul Klein. *L.O.P.* stands for Least Objectionable Programming. The idea is simple: if a show doesn't offend anyone, it will appeal to the widest possible audience. If ABC comes out with a new show about a group of singing fleas—and if that show goes through the roof of Nielsen homes—you can be assured that NBC and CBS will have similar shows in development, faster than you can call an exterminator.

This doesn't mean that new ideas or innovative concepts won't make it to the screen. Each television season brings too many examples of daring shows that break new ground. The fact is, once the ground is broken, the imitation syndrome runs rampant, and we quickly forget that one show was the forerunner of the current trend.

There is no need to write carbon copies of every successful show on television. If a writer has a new idea, it can be presented in a professional format that will be accepted by any production company. A well-written series presentation might convince the reader that the concept has merit, longevity, and the magic ingredient of wide audience appeal. That last element is the most important for the networks. A good television writer learns how to work within those parameters, and does it with genuine creativity and style.

TV Series Formats

Most new ideas for television are submitted in a written presentation called a *format*. The format describes the premise of a show, introduces the characters, and sets the blueprint for action in the series. In the case of an episodic series, the format generally includes the pilot story and future storylines.

If you're planning to create a series, it's helpful to know the identifying characteristics of different series. The most common is the *episodic series,* which features continuing characters in different situations. This is the traditional drama or comedy series with the same running characters facing a different problem each week. The written presentation generally stresses the potential for character conflict, comedy, or suspense. A pilot story provides a clear sense of the action, and storylines for additional episodes may be suggested.

Unlike the episodic series, the *anthology series* (also called a unit series) does *not* have the same characters appearing in each show. The only common thread might be an unusual premise, or the umbrella title of the series itself. The written format for an anthology series might consist of an elaboration of the premise and a detailed outline of the first few shows.

A format can also be written for a *multi-part series*, focusing on one basic story extending over a period of time. This is the framework for the mini-series, often based on book adaptations. The presentation for a multi-part series can be very lengthy and detailed. In that form, it's known as a *bible*, i.e., a thoroughly fleshed-out treatment of characters, story episodes, and creative guidelines.

As we look at formats and how to write them, it might be useful to distinguish between a short program proposal, and a longer series presentation. Although the terms may be used interchangeably, the distinction may clarify some aspects of our discussion. A *preliminary proposal* can be defined as the short conceptual framework for the series; a *presentation* or *bible* is the more completely fleshed-out description of the series.

On the following pages there is a brief proposal—a short format— for a new episodic series called "Together." It's no more than a skeletal outline of the series, with a suggestion of characters and storylines centered around the basic premise.

<u>TOGETHER</u>

It starts as a coincidence. JEREMY WALTERS, 24, bearded and pensive, sits on the steps of the Student Union, watching the rat race go by. RACHEL STONE, 19, fragile and pretty, climbs the steps, and tacks a note on the cluttered bulletin board: "WANTED. RIDE TO EAST COAST."

"I'm going back," JEREMY's voice is friendly, "but I'm hitching." The idea intrigues RACHEL. He's going cross-country at his own pace. To experience change. Adventure. A break from routine. A chance to meet new people in different places. An opportunity to free his spirit.

He's most definitely on RACHEL's vibes.

The groundrules are carefully set up...

The whole thing is on the up and up, platonic and friendly, without any ties. They can stay

in one place for an hour, a day, a week, a month,
depending on their circumstances at the time.
They can split any time they want to--the place
or each other. And when they want to stay some-
where for awhile, or money is low, they pick up
odd jobs, to help support themselves.

That's what our series is about. Two young people
experiencing life to the fullest.

By themselves.

But getting deeply involved in the lives of those
around them.

The sights they see...the places they pass through...
the people they meet...are all key elements of the
series.
We deal with life as it really is...
in the desert...
on the farm...
in small rural towns...
in suburbia...
in the big city.

JEREMY and RACHEL experience it all, and profoundly effect the lives of those whom they meet in the process...

--The teenage hitchhiker, running away from home.

--The old farmer, whose land is threatened by a drought.

--The middle-aged salesman who picks them up, and wants to join them.

--The Vicar, who asks RACHEL to tutor his blind son.

--The owner of the roadside cafe, who was robbed of his savings and accuses JEREMY and RACHEL.

--The alienated little girl whom RACHEL counsels at a small rural summer camp.

--The elderly, frightened woman in a redevelopment project, whose home will be torn down.

In short...

JEREMY AND RACHEL ARE TWO PEOPLE TOGETHER, WHO PROVIDE A RICH SOURCE OF WEEKLY DRAMA, AS THEY BECOME INVOLVED IN A VARIETY OF HUMAN CONFLICTS... WITH DIFFERENT PEOPLE...IN DIFFERENT PLACES... WITH WARM AND SENSITIVE OUTCOMES.

●　　●　　●

You can see that the proposal supplies enough information to convey the basic concept and dramatic potential of the series idea. It uses a combination of narrative techniques and soft-sell approaches (suggesting the reasons why the show might be successful). The brief format offers a sense of the storylines and characters, but it does not provide a detailed visual treatment of the pilot or the leading characters.

A proposal for an anthology series has no running characters to define. Instead, it describes the premise and its basic appeal to viewers. On the following pages you'll find the concept for an anthology proposal, which leans toward the hard-sell approach. It's the format for a supernatural series called "Ghosts!"

GHOSTS!

A Proposal for an Hour Anthology Series

Ghosts. Vampires. Werewolves. Witches.

Ghouls. The very words send ripples up the spine.

There is a deep fascination for the unknown in

each of us. It is an ancient interest--as ancient

as the human race. Therein lies its power. It

is stronger than our intellect, stronger than our

fears. It goes down to the primitive core of our

being.

But the special intrigue of the supernatural

is even more terrifying and fascinating when it

is spiced with recognizable, identifiable people

and places. That is where our series differs from

all others; that is where our series is totally

unique.

"GHOSTS!" is an hour television series that deals with ordinary people from everyday life—confronted with sudden extraordinary events. Some of the events can be explained away. Most cannot!

The unexpected can happen <u>anywhere</u>—under the hair dryer at home; walking down the street in Beverly Hills; eating lunch at Denny's; shopping for gifts at Gimbel's; stopping at the butcher shop in Flatbush; at the grocery store in Austin; riding to work on the Capital Beltway; picking up a date down the block; going to visit your mother-in-law in Maine...

<u>And the unexpected can happen to anyone you know</u>—the young man who walks the dog on your lawn; the old man playing chess in a Greenwich Village park; the woman who goes to a sale at Sear's; the girl you see in the laundromat; the boy who delivers your paper; your blind date for Saturday night...

In fact, it could happen to <u>you</u>. At any place. At any time...

•   •   •

You can see that the written proposal (or brief format) conveys the atmosphere of the potential show and promotes it dramatic *hook*. That *hook* is the show's unique premise. In "Ghosts!" the hook is the intrusion of the supernatural into the lives of identifiable people. In "Together," the hook is less formidable; it is the experience of a young couple hitching cross-country.

A skeletal proposal can run 2–3 pages—as opposed to the more intricately developed series presentation or *bible* which can run 20–100 pages or more.

The Series Presentation: Drama and Comedy

A detailed series presentation reflects the writer's clear grasp of the show's content. It's a much better selling device than the skeletal proposal. Generally, the written presentation for a dramatic or comedy series consists of four separate parts:

1) a *format* section which describes the premise, hook, and appeal of the show;
2) a *character* section which introduces the featured players;
3) a *pilot story* which outlines all the visual sequences for the first episode;
4) a section on *future storylines* which relates story possibilities for additional episodes.

Let's examine the structure and format of each part of the series presentation:

1. The Format Section

As we've already seen, the purpose of a format is to define the concept of the show, briefly and cogently. The style of writing generally reflects the mood and pacing of the proposed show. If the show is a comedy, the format might be warm or slapstick; a drama, poignant and sensitive; action-adventure, fast-paced and action-packed. In short the format whets the reader's appetite for wanting to know more about the series, itself.

The format section usually appears at the beginning of a series presentation. This is the opening segment from a series presentation called "Ziggy's Gang." Shortly we'll examine other segments from this show, as well.

<u>ZIGGY'S GANG</u>

```
ZIGGY'S GANG is a lively half-hour videotape series

for children that captures the early magic of the

"Our Gang" comedies, and the entertaining, educational

qualities of "Sesame Street."
```

The Gang is made up of five lovable, laughable, totally identifiable kids. They are rich, poor, black, and white, representing all shades of personality and character.

The featured characters in ZIGGY'S GANG are a group of friends who go to the same school--a school that cuts across the classes of a medium-sized city, in a neighborhood where extremes live within blocks of one another. The racial and economic mix of the group is never mentioned in the show; it is treated as a simple, natural fact of life. As it should be in real life.

It is ZIGGY'S gang, because ZIGGY is the little human magnet who draws the group together. He is the catalyst that brings out the best in his friends. They care for him, and he cares for them. In fact, they are all inexplicably bound together, and they intend to stay that way, no matter what.

•   •   •

Note that the format is easy to read and describes the fundamental elements of the premise, approach, and character—in a few short paragraphs. Some writers will use separate pages for each paragraph or two, making the presentation appear even more spacious. That's simply a matter of style and preference.

Here's the format page from a new action-adventure series called "Intercept." The entire premise is described in less than a page.

INTERCEPT

FORMAT

INTERCEPT IS A NEW TWIST ON AN ACTION-ADVENTURE IDEA.

IT TEAMS AN AMERICAN GIRL WITH A JAPANESE GUY, IN AN ATTEMPT

TO THWART INTERNATIONAL CRIMINALS.

THE MOOD OF THE SERIES? -- TONGUE IN CHEEK ADVENTURE.

THE TWIST?

OUR TWO LEADS ARE EXPERTS IN THE MARTIAL ARTS. AND THE ARTS

ARE DEPICTED IN MORE DETAIL THAN EVER BEFORE. KARATE. AIKIDO.

BATON TECHNIQUE. THEY ARE USED IN HIGHLY STYLIZED SEQUENCES

EACH WEEK -- WITHOUT GRATUITOUS VIOLENCE. AND WITH A SENSE OF

EXCITEMENT AND ENTERTAINMENT.

• • •

Note that the information in the "Intercept" format is basically the same as "Ziggy's Gang." The concept of the series is presented, the atmosphere suggested, and the hook briefly delineated. However, the style of writing is different, and the form of presentation is different— all the information is double-spaced and capitalized in this presentation. In writing program formats, there is plenty of room for diversity and experimentation. The most important objective is to lay the dramatic groundwork, and evoke interest in the series idea.

2. Characters

Leading characters in an episodic series can be described simply —looks, age, key character traits, potential interrelationships in the series. The characters can be developed more fully in the pilot story. (Character development is discussed in Part Two.)

The number of leading characters can be relatively small. Some producers instinctively translate a long list of characters into a massive price tag for casting. In "Ziggy's Gang" there are five characters—an unusually large number for this section of the presentation—but each one is considered integral to the premise and pilot story. This is how they are described:

ZIGGY

You can't help but love ZIGGY. He's an eleven year old chubby kid with big, wire-rimmed glasses, floppy blonde hair, and a cherubic baby face. He's the eternal optimist who is momentarily crushed when things don't work out his way. But he latches onto a new hope, and his enthusiasm waxes incredibly high again. ZIGGY's warm-heartedness and undaunted spirit spark his friends to want to help set things right; no matter how outlandish the scheme. ZIGGY's the son of a college professor, and he gets his share of jibes about it at school. He's idealistic, enthusiastic, and adventuresome; he's sensitive, too, with a heart of pure gold.

DUDE

DUDE dazzles you. He is a "with-it" ten year old hustler who talks cool and moves cool. DUDE knows all the angles and uses them to help his friends at all costs. He is a loyal friend, with a sincerity that outlasts his "con-man" exterior. His impetuous "cons" are responsible for getting the gang into trouble and sometimes are the cause of disharmony and misunderstanding within the gang itself. DUDE is the flamboyant son of a blue collar worker; he lives several blocks away from ZIGGY.

SAMSON

SAMSON's got to make you laugh. He's a short, wiry eleven year old, with a tremendous sense of humor and an outlandish laugh. Smaller than the others, he prides himself on being a tremendous athlete. His speed, agility and strength helped earn him a "tough boy" reputation. (The reputation was aided and abetted by DUDE, who has everyone convinced that SAMSON is a karate expert.) SAMSON has one major flaw--a hot temper that occasionally clouds his sense of humor. Inevitably, it gets the gang into trouble when it surfaces. SAMSON is forced to take trombone lessons in which he has no interest or talent. He's utterly embarassed on those days he has to lug his oversized instrument to school.

BUCKS

You have to feel sorry for BUCKS. He's a tall, lanky thirteen year old rich kid. He's prone to day-dreaming and fantasy, which gives him an affinity for his younger friends. BUCKS is the bumbler of the group. The son of a corporation president, he lives in an expensive high-rise apartment and refuses to

take a large allowance from his parents. BUCKS yearns
to be "poor," like the rest of the kids.

LADY

    LADY makes you stop, look, and listen. She's the
only one with both feet on the ground. She may be
only twelve years old, but she's got more than her
share of common-sense and book-sense. (She's brilliant
in the sciences, and can do wonders with anything
mechanical). LADY is Latin American with long jet
black hair, big brown eyes, and a full, rich, happy
smile. She finds herself caught between the good
times she has as a tomboy, and the good times she's
beginning to have as a full-fledged, female,
feminine girl. LADY is often razzed by the others
since she represents the lone, stable, level-headed
point of view. She is the daughter of a neighborhood grocery store owner.

●   ●   ●

The character descriptions can be even shorter. In this presentation for the "Intercept" series, the two lead characters were defined in a
sentence or two:

SANDY FELTON, 22, from West Los Angeles, beautiful and intelligent.
She looks more like a fashion model than she does a third degree
black belt.

<u>SHIHAN</u> <u>TAKAYUKI</u> <u>KUBOTA</u> ("Mr. K.", for short), 35, from Japan, a

quiet powerhouse of a man, no more than 5'3". He is an accomplished

Master of the Oriental Martial Arts.

●   ●   ●

Again, the writing style for character description depends on the specific needs of the show and pilot story.

3. Pilot Stories and Treatments

Pilot stories have little time to accomplish everything the writer has in mind, so be selective and sparing in development. The *treatment* is a narrative version of the story concept. It can provide the right atmosphere, visually and emotionally, giving the reader a full sense of characters, place, and action. The characters and conflicts are usually introduced as early as possible, and the dramatic builds are carefully orchestrated from beginning to end. In Part Two there is a discussion of dramatic theory and story plotting techniques, essential to effective development. At this point, however, let's just look at the technical requirements and formal structure of an original treatment.

A pilot story can be segmented into several acts. A half-hour program usually has a brief "teaser" followed by two acts of equal length. A sixty-minute show might have a teaser and four acts. A two-hour project might have six acts—or none at all. These are general guidelines, of course, rather than formal requisites.

As for professional jargon, relatively little is called for. These are some of the recurring terms or directions that might appear in a pilot story or treatment:

FADE IN: This means that the picture gradually appears onto the screen. Conversely, at the end of a story or script, the picture FADES OUT and the screen goes to black.

EXT. PARK—DAY: This is called a "slug line" or "identification line" because it spells out the different scene locations in the story. It identifies the location as exterior (EXT.) or interior (INT.), specifies the place of the action (PARK), and the lighting requirements (DAY or NIGHT). Scripts are broken down this way to help identify production elements in the show. In the story phase there is some variance about the use of slug lines. Some writers will omit them altogether, preferring a more narrative style in the treatment. The specific form is up to the individual writer.

O.S.: This is a shorthand way of saying "Off Screen." If a character sees something off screen, it means the viewer can't see what he or she is looking at.

HIS P.O.V.: This means we are now looking from the character's "point of view." We see exactly what that person sees.

CU: This means "Close Up." The close up is a camera shot that features a large image on screen.

On the following pages you'll find the pilot treatment for "Ziggy's Gang." Let's examine the technical structure of the first act:

PILOT STORY ← *The Title of the pilot goes here*

Stories and scripts usually begin with this direction

FADE IN:

The "slug line" (or scene identification) may be used in the treatment or may be discarded

EXT. PARK--DAY

The Gang is involved in a hot game of basketball

Characters are often capitalized throughout

at the park. ZIGGY, jaunting down the side of the

court, has a clear path to the basket, but suddenly

stops short as he sees something O.S. SAMSON

Off-screen

passes the ball, but ZIGGY is oblivious, and the

ball bounces off him. SAMSON groans with exasper-

ation, but ZIGGY continues to stare O.S.

a new angle from his point-of-view

HIS P.O.V.

He's staring at the new girl in his class, SANDY

HOLLANDER, blonde and pretty, who is talking and

joking with thirteen year old "Adonis," BILLY

MATLICK. They're sitting on the grass together.

double spacing suggests new angles or scenes

BILLY sees the ball bounce off the court, and

he gets up to retrieve it. He gets the ball and

tries a shot from way off the court... He "swishes"
it through the hoop. SANDY is delighted and im-
pressed, BILLY smiles proudly, and ZIGGY doesn't
react at all. From the sidelines, LADY is the
only one who seems to take stock of the situation.

The action in the sequence is described without using specific camera angles

EXT. STREET--DAY ← *(This sets a new place, a new scene)*

DUDE, SAMSON, and BUCKS are entering the garage,
but ZIGGY sees someone coming down the street,
and purposely lags behind. It's SANDY, with BILLY
in tow. ZIGGY greets them awkwardly, and sees
that she's carrying a new album...It's by her
favorite rock star, and BILLY just bought it for
her...She goes on about how unexpected the gift
was, how unnecessary it was for BILLY to spend
four dollars like that, for no reason at all...
BILLY smiles. It was nothing, he says. And they
exit, leaving ZIGGY gawking after them. Almost
instinctively, he digs into his pocket and pulls
out some change. He doesn't have nearly enough
to compete.

In a treatment Dialogue is merely suggested

LADY arrives on her bike, stands it up by the
garage, and apologizes for being late. She
quizzically notes ZIGGY's tormented look as he
heads quietly for the garage. She looks after
him for a beat, then glances down the street,
where she sees SANDY walking with BILLY. So
that's it, she guesses.

[handwritten note, with arrow to circled "beat":] A "BEAT" is a dramatic pause

INT. GARAGE--DAY

Inside the garage, BUCKS asks ZIGGY what's wrong,
why is he so down? It's so unlike him...It's
nothing, ZIGGY says. But LADY enters, and offers
another theory...It's nothing to be ashamed of...
ZIGGY is taken with that new girl in class...
SANDY HOLLANDER...The guys break into hoots,
catcalls, general razzing...ZIGGY gets red-faced
denies it, and begins to storm out.

[handwritten note:] once again, dialogue is implied without using actual dialogue structure

LADY shouts for the others to lay off...They stop.
DUDE says the new chick is BILLY MATLICK'S, and
there ain't nobody, no how, gonna get the li'l fox

from BILLY-THE-KID...The others agree whole-
heartedly...LADY again chimes in, tells them
that instead of razzing ZIGGY, or telling him
how hopeless it is, they ought to think of
something that might help...It would take a <u>lot</u>
to help, ZIGGY says half-resignedly, that
BILLY kid is even rich. He just bought her a
new album.

All eyes turn at once to BUCKS--who looks
horror-stricken. But ZIGGY jumps in immediately,
says no to that idea...You know how BUCKS hates
to take money from his dad. There <u>must</u> be
another way...BUCKS looks like a ten ton
weight was just removed from his shoulders.

Then SAMSON's eyes light up. He has an idea...
What about getting back at BILLY on the court,
and impressing the chick?...SAMSON can teach him
everything he has to know. He doesn't have to
be big, or handsome, or tall, or strong to beat
BILLY in basketball...It's all in the moves,

[handwritten note in right margin:] The pilot story should be detailed enough to give a complete sense of time, place, action, and character development in each major sequence

man, and ZIGGY can <u>take</u> him in a one-on-one

game...ZIGGY becomes enthused. ZIGGY, the

eternal optimist, agrees to give it a try.

The others cheer him on.

> *Instead of using the slug line, the writer may opt for a narrative style, e.g., "We are outside the garage and see that SAMSON is teaching ZIGGY..."etc.*

<u>EXT. GARAGE--DAY</u>

SAMSON is teaching ZIGGY the moves and the shots,

using a meg-shift hoop the gang set up in front

of the garage. SAMSON purposely lets ZIGGY

get by him, and ZIGGY, after two misses, finally

hits a bucket. The gang cheers wildly, and

SAMSON smiles...You're ready, ZIGGY-boy. You'll

beat him so bad, she'll be begging for an auto-

graph...ZIGGY beams, as SAMSON runs out to

arrange the match.

> *In the pilot story, a writer can use either of these approaches to indicate a new scene*

<u>EXT. PARK--DAY</u>   *(and/or)*

In the park, we see the kids gathering around

the basketball court, filtering in, jabbering

about the match. Finally, the crowd quiets

down as BILLY strolls calmly out on the court

in his school team sweatshirt, and his brand

new thirty-dollar All-pro basketball shoes.   Two

shots for warm-up; two swishes.

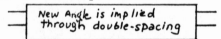

New Angle is implied through double-spacing

ZIGGY strolls out onto the court now.   His chunky

belly and short frame seem to belie his sense of

calm and confidence.   BILLY hands him the ball

for his warm-up shots, but ZIGGY declines.   BILLY

asks ZIGGY to take the ball out, but again ZIGGY

gives him the advantage.   Some buzzing from the

crowd.   SANDY, on the grass, watches.

New Angle implied

The game is on, and cheers from the rooting

sections accompany the action.   BILLY dribbles

behind his back, and ZIGGY looks momentarily

confused.   BILLY drives in, and ZIGGY falls down.

An easy lay-up for two.

This is the viewer's point of view

ZIGGY tries to dribble behind his back, but

trips over the ball. Laughter, cheers, and groans

from the crowd.   SAMSON and the others in the

gang pass worried looks back and forth.   We can

see that SANDY feels sorry for ZIGGY, but she

roots for BILLY.

The scene description can define Continuous action or Compressed action

The game continues...BILLY looking like Pistol

Pete, and ZIGGY looking like Oliver Hardy. As

the game draws to an end, the Gang knows it's

a totally lost cause. BILLY tosses in the last

bucket, and steps over the exhausted, nearly

prone body of ZIGGY. As the Gang forlornly moves

in to see ZIGGY, BILLY moves back toward the

sidelines to see SANDY.

his point of view can be Specified where necessary

From (ZIGGY's P.O.V.) we see the triumphant BILLY

being greeted with a hero's welcome. He puts

his arm around SANDY's shoulder, and they walk

off.

CLOSE-UPS are one of the few shots called in a treatment. They can help establish a character's reaction to emotional crises or specific events unfolding.

CU ZIGGY's reaction. We see how crushed he is.

This slug line establishes a new scene and location

EXT. STREET--DAY

ZIGGY walks despondently back toward the garage,

with a silent Gang following along. Then DUDE

thrusts his arm around ZIGGY, and says as only

DUDE can say...Hey, Man, he may be a sportin'
dude, and he may be richer and taller and better
lookin' than you, but nobody say that dude's
cool. And that's what you gonna be, ZIG, Man,
you gonna be cool...ZIGGY looks curiously up at
DUDE's smiling face, and the light of optimism
begins to cross his features again.

Implied dialogue is sprinkled in the treatment

and so are reactions

INT. GARAGE--DAY

This is the final dress rehearsal. ZIGGY wears
some far-out clothes, and is finishing up his
jive-talk speech to DUDE, who plays the part of
SANDY. DUDE smiles and says in a high-pitched
feminine voice...Oh, you so cool, ZIGGY, you
be my new sweetie-man...ZIGGY beams from ear to
ear. And just then we hear the distant sound of
SANDY's (O.S.) laughter. She's going to pass by
the garage on her way home from school. DUDE
looks at ZIGGY and gives him the power sign...
You ready, Man...ZIGGY rushes out of the garage
to meet her.

"off-screen"

EXT. STREET--DAY

ZIGGY stands in front of the open garage, trying

to look inconspicuous. We see SANDY and BILLY

walking down the street towards him. ZIGGY

whispers out loud to DUDE, hidden in the shadows

of the garage...She's with BILLY...DUDE reinforces

his friend's confidence...Don't worry, Man. When

you get through, the li'l fox'll be like ice

cream in summer, in your hands.

Implied dialogue

As SANDY and BILLY approach, ZIGGY struts out and

lays his line on them. The words are right, but

they sound like they're being read from a text-

book. The strut, the moves, and the dress, make

ZIGGY look more like a stand up comic than a cool

ladies' man. BILLY starts cracking up, becomes

hysterical. SANDY tries hard not to laugh, asks

ZIGGY why he's acting so funny...Laughing, BILLY

tugs SANDY's arm, and they continue on their way.

an EXTREME CLOSE-UP

In (an ECU,) we see how totally crushed and embar-

assed ZIGGY is.

This direction generally ends each act and concludes each film

FADE OUT

● ● ●

As mentioned earlier, a writer doesn't have to conform to this style of writing the treatment. A looser, more narrative style omits the need for formal scene identifications. All the information is given in visual description, and new scenes are suggested by setting up new paragraphs. Here is an example of the more narrative approach. It is an excerpt from the "Intercept" pilot. The action picks up as Kubota, a martial arts expert, escapes from his captors.

KUBOTA bolts down the darkened hallway toward a

SECOND GUARD, who turns clumsily with his shot

gun.. But KUBOTA does a flying leap kick, knocks

the gun out of the man's hands.

In the narrative format, a paragraph establishes the place of a scene. There is no need for a slug line

Now he races down the courthouse hallway, toward

the elevator. He frantically forces the doors

open.

The writer can still use a specific point of view

His P.O.V.--The elevator shaft is a black empty

abyss. Far below him a light seeps through one

of the lower floors.

This is a new scene

special effects are capitalized

KUBOTA has no choice. He leaps into the elevator

shaft, grabbing the cable, and descends rapidly

hand over hand...SUDDENLY we HEAR the SOUND of the

elevator motor starting up, echoing, pulsating

below him. The elevator starts to rise...Above

him he sees the GUARD with the shotgun prying

open the doors. He's caught in the middle.

point of view is suggested

Using the elevator as a swinging vine, he leaps

over to the side of the shaft, bumping against the

second floor exit door. He reaches for the metal

handle of the exit and forces the door open--

just as the elevator itself is about to trap him.

> This is actually a new scene - "INT. OFFICE - DAY"
> But it is not necessary to identify it in the
> narrative format

He lets himself out.. into a big office filled

with desks and secretaries, other clerical types.

They pay no attention to him as he casually walks

from the elevator exit to the front entrance...

nodding amicably to a person or two...as he disap-

pears out the front door.

● ● ●

4. Future Storylines

Even with a strong pilot story, producers are inclined to ask: "Where does it go from here?" They have an inordinate fear that pilot stories are one shots; that series longevity can't be achieved. That's what this section—Future Storylines—is about.

In no more than a few paragraphs you might convince the producer that the potential for series episodes is virtually unlimited. You can provide a number of different storylines (6–13 on the average) showing the built-in diversity of the concept and character interaction. Each story area can reflect the potential for dramatic conflict.

The following storylines show how the "Ziggy's Gang" series might be developed in future episodes. The storylines are brief—a single paragraph with a beginning, middle, and end. Since the featured characters were already described in the presentation, and the pilot story showed them in action, the producer already has an idea of how they might act and react in these types of stories. These are just three out of thirteen future storylines for the show:

Future Storylines

1. ZIGGY is running for a school office, and the gang converts the garage into temporary campaign headquarters. The opponent is a fast-talking charmer who looks like a shoo-in. DUDE tries to teach ZIGGY how to out-talk his opponent, but ZIGGY knows he can't do it. As the campaign gets underway, he decides to be himself and suffer the consequences -- but the gang plays up his honesty and "down home sincerity", and ZIGGY wins in an upset victory.

2. There's a talent show at the park, and the gang wants to win the trophy. They enter SAMSON as a trombone player, who, of course, wants nothing to do with it. But he acquiesces for the gang's sake. He's terrible and loses. The gang realizes he did his best, and sacrificed his own desires on their behalf -- so they build a trophy of their own, and present it to him in their own garage.

3. LADY is being pursued by a boy at school. She tells everyone she wants to get rid of him, he's a pest, a nuisance. Her reaction is so strong, the gang tries to discourage the boy -- until they realize LADY really likes him. They recognize that LADY is not only one of the guys, she's one of the girls, too. They do their best to set things right.

●　●　●

The storylines can be written in separate paragraphs as they appear above, or on separate pages for each story. Once all the storylines are written, the writer can take time to embellish some, delete others, or add additional stories for the sake of series longevity and dramatic diversity.

3

The Variety Special and Quiz Show

The Variety Special

A television special requires a totally different approach from the weekly series presentation. The appeal of the show is generally based on the event itself—soccer championships, Bermuda Triangle mysteries, the backstage antics of shooting a feature film. By definition, a special is designed to be a one shot competitive entry for the networks or syndicated market.

A proposal for a variety special generally centers around the star and the package. A *package* is a strong line-up of creative talent committed to the show (actors, singers, musicians, dancers, directors, producers). At this stage of development, it may be too early to seek actual commitments, but it is possible to assess individual intents and interest. Even with that, every variable under the sun may affect the producer's ability to deliver a package—from availability dates and conflicts, to negotiations over salaries and screen credits.

It's highly unlikely that an unestablished writer will be called upon to write a special. Still it's helpful to know the way a special is developed, and the way it might be packaged.

Assume, if you will, that the network is looking for a variety special in the fall, and that you have some connections in the variety field. Since specials sell on the basis of concept and packages, here is a sample proposal that might start the ball rolling.

HOLLYWOOD IN VEGAS

A Music Special With Nancy and Frank Sinatra, Jr.

OUR TOUR GUIDES...NANCY AND FRANK SINATRA, JR.

THEY TAKE US ALL OVER HOLLYWOOD AND VEGAS, SINGING AND MINGLING WITH THE BEST...

HELEN REDDY IN VEGAS...THE ROLLING STONES AT A HOLLYWOOD RECORDING SESSION...LIZA MINELLI IN CONCERT...HENRY WINKLER ON A PROMO TOUR...

THEY GO TOGETHER, SING TOGETHER, PLAY TOGETHER, EVEN AT A MEN'S ONLY CLUB, WHERE DON RICKLES IS THE ROAST MASTER.

THIS SPECIAL IS ONE THAT WILL BE REMEMBERED. EVEN BY PAPA FRANK SINATRA, SR., WHO PAYS A SURPRISE VISIT AT THE END.

THIS SPECIAL IS A FAMILY AFFAIR IN EVERY SENSE OF THE WORD!

●　　●　　●

If the stars agree to the premise, the creator needs to line up some other heavyweights, including a strong producer-director. The creator also needs to provide a *Rundown Sheet* which delineates show segments and the expected timing for each segment. The timing is generally broken down into Seg Time (segment time) and Run Time. *Seg*

Time refers to the length of individual segments in the show; whereas *Run Time* is the accumulated timing for the entire program. Once the project actually goes into rehearsals, the timing is modified to fit the actual production requirements of the show.

This is what a sample rundown sheet looks like:

"HOLLYWOOD IN VEGAS" RUNDOWN

Seg.			Seg Time	Run Time
I.				
	A.	Frank and Nancy at home, opening patter and intro. (:50)		
	B.	First Song: Nancy & Frank (2:24)	3:14	3:14
		COMMERCIAL	1:04	4:18
II.				
	A.	Frank & Nancy prep for concert with Helen Reddy (:17)		
	B.	Helen Reddy sings in concert (3:14)		
	C.	Frank & Nancy joke in concert (1:00)		
	D.	Helen joins Frank & Nancy for medley (4:34)	9:05	13:23
		COMMERCIAL	1:04	14:27
III.				
	A.	Prep for joining Henry Winkler on promo tour (:07)		
	B.	Henry's patter on tour, comedy bit (2:14)		
	C.	Nancy & Frank intro Henry doing Shakespeare (:42)		
	D.	Henry Winkler does Shakespeare (3:29)		
	E.	Henry joins Nancy & Frank for song (2:34)	9:06	23:33
		COMMERCIAL	1:04	24:37

"HOLLYWOOD IN VEGAS" RUNDOWN
(Continued)

Seq			Seg Time	Run Time
IV.				
	A.	Frank & Nancy patter, heading toward recording session (:20)		
	B.	Intro Rolling Stones, who have the studio before them (:13)		
	C.	The Stones do medley in studio (6:40)		
	D.	Nancy & Frank record their songs (3:32)	10:45	35:22
		COMMERCIAL	1:04	36:26
V.				
	A.	Frank & Nancy patter; Don Rickles invites them to appear with him at unnamed club (:30)		
	B.	Nancy arrives at club: A Men's Only (:10)		
	C.	Rickles does comedy routine (4:03)		
	D.	Nancy & Frank join in comedy bit (2:23)	7:06	43:32
		COMMERCIAL	1:04	44:36
VI.				
	A.	Prep for night's concert with Liza Minelli (:11)		
	B.	Liza sings medley in concert (3:43)		
	C.	Liza, Frank, and Nancy sing (2:40)	6:34	51:10

"HOLLYWOOD IN VEGAS" RUNDOWN
(Continued)

Seg			Seg Time	Run Time
		COMMERCIAL	1:04	52:14
VII.				
	A.	Nancy's solo number (2:10)		
	B.	Frank's solo number (2:30)		
	C.	Frank & Nancy at home, surprise appearance, Frank Sinatra, Sr. (:45)		
	D.	Frank & Nancy's Goodnights to audience (:20)		
	E.	Credits (:38)	6:23	58:37

• • •

If a production company or a network wants a more detailed presentation, they might set a deal to put the project together. Variety proposals are usually short and sketchy, to test the waters for a nibble. Until you have strong connections and a good track record, it will be a hard sale to make.

The Quiz Program Proposal

In the world of television writing, *comedy-variety* programs include quiz or audience participation shows. The proposal for a quiz show is an entity unto itself. The narrative is a combination of hard-sell and practical description. It conveys the excitement of the show, while it answers questions about the format, set design, and production values.

Here's the program proposal for a quiz show called "Compute-a-Quiz." Note how it describes the format and production requirements, while it offers an on-going sense of the show and it's pacing.

COMPUTE-A-QUIZ

COMPUTE-A-QUIZ IS AN EXCITING HALF-HOUR GAME
SHOW FOR CHILDREN, WHICH STIMULATES THE MIND
AND CHALLENGES THE REFLEXES. IT'S AS FAST-
PACED AS A MODERN DAY COMPUTER.

IN EACH SHOW, THE CONTESTANTS--AGES 6-12--
VIE FOR A WIDE RANGE OF PRIZES, FROM CREATIVE
PLAYTHINGS TO EXPENSE-PAID TRIPS TO DISNEY-
LAND. THE FINAL GRAND PRIZE OF THE DAY IS
AWARDED IN THE SHOPPING-HALL-OF-THE-FUTURE,
WHERE THE TOTAL PRIZE POINTS ARE COMPUTED.

THE FORMAT

Our M. C. introduces two contestants to the
audience, asks them about their background,
their age, school, and interests. Now the
game begins.

The contestants are seated on futuristic
podiums, facing a giant, stylized computer
screen. They have "compute-a-control boards"
which activate a circle of flashing lights
on the screen. The contestant who first
flashes the lights, answers the question.

If the answer is right, the computer counts
out the prize points. If the answer is wrong,
the computer "fizzles." Our M. C. gives the
right answer, then it's on to the next question.

Our program is keyed to a lightning fast inquiry
of general knowledge, and is climaxed by the
"Compute-a-Point Shopping Spree." Once the
points are accumulated, the contestants enter
the shopping hall of the future, where they
can select any number of prizes--so long as
they stay within range of their computer prize
points.

SAMPLE QUESTIONS

COMPUTE-A-QUIZ questions are designed to test
general knowledge as well as academic prowess.
And they come in any form...

    VISUAL. On the computer screen, itself...

    AURAL. Heard through the computer speaker...

    TOSS-UP. Direct from the M. C.

The questions appear in haphazard combinations,
keeping contestants and viewers on their toes.

On the computer screen we see a horse, a chicken,
a cow. The M. C. asks· "Which is a member of
the fowl family?"

Two voices are heard through the computer speaker.
The M. C. asks: "Which of those voices is the
President of the United States?"

On the screen, we see a rectangle, a triangle,
a square, and a circle. The screen goes blank,
and the M. C. asks: "Which shape came before
the triangle?"

On the screen, we see an apple, a pear, and a
lemon. The M.C. asks: "Which of these are fruit?"
The contestant must name them all in order to win.

We hear a train whistle, a coach's whistle, a
clarinet, and a tug boat. The M. C. asks: "Which
is used by a football coach?"

On the screen, we see the numbers: 0,2,4,5. The
M. C. asks: "Which can be divided by two?"

We hear the computer whirr, and see the lights
flash. From the speaker we hear a lion's roar,
a dog's bark, a cat's meow. The M. C. asks:
"Which belong to the feline family?" The respon-
dent has to name the cat and the lion to win.

•   •   •

The quiz proposal deals with the genre enthusiastically and tries to
provide a "live" sense of the show. The proposal can be submitted to
any successful quiz show producer, videotape production house, or
television packager. The actual submission process for new projects is
discussed in Part Four of this book.

•   •   •

Now that you're familiar with various formats for commercial
series and specials, it's time to look at non-commercial alternatives.
Some projects might fit exceptionally well into the public television
mode. Even if you have limited interest in the non-commercial area at
the moment, you might find the marketplace unusually relevant for
other projects that you might develop.

4

Public TV Presentations

The Public Television Marketplace

America's system of public television was originaly inspired by a report of the Carnegie Commission on Educational Television, published as *Public Television: A Program for Action* *. Twelve years later that system of program development, financing, production, and distribution underwent a probing re-examination. The Carnegie Commission on the Future of Public Broadcasting undertook an eighteen month study, hearing testimony from TV writers, producers, station managers, and others involved in public broadcasting. That 1979 report found the system fraught with weaknesses—from political in-fighting to lack of funds for significant creative development †.

As a result of this latest study the Commission recommended the establishment of a new national entity—The Public Telecommunications Trust—which would replace the Corporation for Public Broadcasting (CPB). In essence, the Trust would be responsible for national leadership, planning, and development in the entire public television realm. One of its chief functions would be to house and protect a most important Division from outside pressures: The Program Services Endowment.

The Program Services Endowment is conceived as the central agency for increasing public television's commitment to American writers and producers. According to the Carnegie Commission, this

---

Public Television: A Program for Action, New York: Harper & Row, 1967.
†*A Public Trust: The Report of the Carnegie Commission on the Future of Public Broadcasting.* New York: Bantam Books, 1979.

Endowment would have a single objective—to support the American creative community and the development of qualitative programs.

The Commission's recommendations will undoubtedly have a profound effect on the current marketplace. It prescribes $1.2 billion annually for public broadcasting by 1985, and encourages freelance writers and producers to create shows without undue pressures or influences. To help you wade through the maze of federal support for TV writers and producers, here is a rundown of the most relevant agencies as they function at the time of printing.

PBS and CPB

The most familiar entities are PBS (the Public Broadcasting Service) and CPB (the Corporation for Public Broadcasting). PBS is the representative agency of all local public broadcasting stations. It arranges for distribution of new programs on the public television network, and is concerned with national, regional, and target audience broadcasts. PBS helps develop some programming, but is primarily concerned with program distribution.

While PBS acts as a developer and distributor, CPB has traditionally functioned as a developer and funding source. The Corporation offers financial backing for script development and production. In the past they've allocated several hundred million each year on the production of pilots, series, and specials (usually in association with other funding agencies). In early 1980, CPB was structurally revamped along Program Endowment lines, modeled after the Carnegie Commission Report. One part of the Corporation now deals exclusively with management services, while the other deals with the Program Fund—a funding source devoted exclusively to the development and production of programs for public broadcasting.

CPB has been increasingly interested in reaching the largest possible audiences with innovative shows. They feel that programs with wider audience appeal provide a greater return for the taxpayer's dollar. They've been open to program ideas from Hollywood producers as well as freelance writers. If you have a possible project for public television, you can write for the guidelines from CPB (1111 16th St., N.W., Washington, D.C. 20036). If you don't have a strong track record, it might help to submit the proposal through a public television station or an established production company.

NEA and NEH

Two of the more important federal agencies which support new television projects are the National Endowment for the Arts (*NEA*) and the National Endowment for the Humanities (*NEH*), both headquartered in Washington, D.C. Each year Congress allocates hundreds of millions of dollars to both Endowments for the support of cultural and artistic projects in this country. Both agencies have a Media Program for the support of creative and relevant television and film projects.

National Endowment for the Arts

Not long ago, NEA supported projects that dealt exclusively with the cultural arts. Now they have expanded the ground rules to include any project of high artistic merit. The rationale is quite bold and admirable: TV, film, and radio are recognized as artistic media in their own right, and they can provide a range of quality-oriented programming to the nation. The Media Arts Program usually offers matching funds up to $50,000 for individual projects. The "matching funds" requirement is important; that means the writer or producer must find additional underwriting sources to supplement the NEA grant.

In addition to production grants, NEA supports writers and producers through various fellowship programs. One of the programs is administered through the American Film Institute (AFI) and is for the development and production of fiction, documentary, animation, and experimental films. A description of the program and formal applications can be obtained from the American Film Institute, 501 Doheny Drive, Beverly Hills, California 90210.

In the area of documentaries, NEA and the Ford Foundation jointly sponsor fellowships for writers and producers. The Television Laboratory at WNET-TV in New York administers that program. Their address: WNET, 356 West 58th St., New York, N.Y. 10019.

A separate Literature Program at NEA also supports writers through a creative writing fellowship. Although no mention of television is specifically made in their announcement, the program *does* support the writing of original TV or film scripts. To determine eligibility and application requirements, contact the Literature Program, NEA, Washington, D.C. 20506.

The National Endowment for the Humanities

NEH is the other major funding agency. The Division of Public Programs is particularly relevant to freelance television writers and independent producers. It supports the development and production of new television, film, and radio projects with outright grants ranging from $10,000 to several million dollars. The Media Program at NEH has funded such television projects as "Odyssey," "The Scarlet Letter," "The Adams Chronicles," "The Best of Families," "The American Short Story," and many others of high merit.

The NEH Media Program encourages professional writers and producers to work in cooperation with scholars in particular program areas. The meeting-of-the-minds between professionals and scholars creates a challenging atmosphere, and contributes to some mutually rewarding ideas about program development in the humanities.

NEH offers several types of grants: 1) *Planning grants* support writers, producers, and scholars seeking to develop innovative media humanities projects. 2) *Script Development grants* are the most relevant for television writers, since they are designed to support the writing of scripts and series outlines. They cover appropriate research costs (travel, consultants, etc.) as well as development costs (writer's fees, story conferences, typing and duplicating, etc.). These grants might range from $20,000 to over $100,000, with no requirements for matching funds (*i.e.,* it is an outright grant to the writer or project director). 3) *Production grants* can be for single programs, pilots, or series episodes. These can range from $100,000 to over $1 million or more, and can include the development of additional scripts. Since these grants are so costly, they usually require additional gifts and matching funds from other sources.

As for submission of proposals, NEH strongly recommends a preliminary inquiry at least six weeks before each deadline. The staff can help determine the appropriateness of the project and can help you to prepare a more competitive proposal for submission. In addition, staff can guide the project through formal evaluation procedures. A complete description of relevant grant programs, proposal requirements, and application deadlines are available in *Media Guidelines,* Division of Public Programs, National Endowment for the Humanities, Washington, D.C. 20506.

There is another program within NEH that might be of special interest to young writers and producers. The *Youthgrants in the Humanities* program is designed specifically for students and young people (under 30) who want to relate the humanities to public audiences. This seems to be an excellent source for young writers who would like to explore the media in important and innovative ways. The appropriate guidelines are available from the Endowment, along with a description of the Youthgrants program.

Other Funding Sources

There are other federal funding sources for non-commercial television programs. For example, U.S. Office of Education subsidized "Sesame Street" and ESSA-TV (Emergency Secondary School Act) subsidized "Que Pasa." Such federal agencies usually publish *RFP's*— Requests for Proposals—outlining their respective needs and objectives for new television programs. The *RFP's* invite competitive submissions of program concepts. All *RFP's* are announced in *Commerce Business Daily* (the non-commercial equivalent of *Daily Variety* and *The Hollywood Reporter*).

Unfortunately there are hundreds of irrelevant proposals published; it is difficult and time-consuming to find one that will interest you. A combined listing of *RFP's* is published in the *Federal Domestic Assistance Catalogue,* which offers detailed information about each competitive submission. Perhaps the most useful source is the *Federal Funding Update,* an informal publication of the Public Broadcasting System, summarizing grant deadlines and relevant RFP activities for writers, producers and station managers.

In addition to federal support, there are private foundations that offer grants and awards to television writers and producers. For a complete listing of these resources, see the *Annotated Bibliography* at the back of this book; it includes material on a wide-range of funding sources and activities. In addition, you'll find a directory of "Federal Agencies, Private Foundations, and Public Television Associations" in the *Appendix.*

Proposal Writing for Non-Commercial Television

If you're planning to submit a project to any public agency, first write for the guidelines and application forms. The guidelines will give you a broad idea of the agency's needs, and your proposal will have to address those needs. A public television proposal is generally comprised of three parts: 1) the formal application (called the "Face Sheet"); 2) the narrative proposal which details your objectives and program format; 3) the budget. In addition, a timetable is usually included, and the vitae (resumés) of all key personnel are included.

The Face Sheet

The first page of the formal application is called a Face Sheet. It asks for identifying information about the applicant and the proposal. Most Face Sheets require an abstract to be written in a paragraph or two, outlining the objectives and format of the show. It also asks for information about key personnel. A carefully worded synopsis is especially important when you consider the fact that some evaluators might only see that first page abstract.

A sample Face Sheet appears on the next page. There are *many* variations on the same theme, depending on the agency's individual forms.

NEH — APPLICATION COVER SHEET

Form OMB-128-R-0071

1. Individual.Applicant/Principal Project Director
a. Name and Mailing Address

Sprager,   Hart
(last,   first,   initial)

Spectrum IV Productions

Austin,   Texas 78702
(city)   (state)   (zip)

President
title/position

f. Telephone
(512 -- -- ext.

g. Citizenship
1. ☒ USA 2. ☐ Other Specify:

b. Date of Birth
-- / -/ --
mo day year

c. Major Field of Study
--

d. Highest Degree Attained
--   -/ --
mo year

e. Education
--

(For NEH use ONLY)

Date Received   /   /
Application #
Initials

2. Type of Application
1. ☒ New   2. ☐ Revision
*3. ☐ Renewal *4. ☐ Supplement
*If 3 or 4 (above) enter previous grant #

4. Type of Applicant

1. ☐ Individual

*2. ☒ Institution/Organization

* If (2) above (inst./org.) enter -
Type: TV Production
Status: Private

3. Program To Which Application Is Being Made

Media Program

5. Requested Period   Total Months
3/15/82   9/15/82=   6
From: mo day yr   To: mo day yr

6. Audiences (Direct Beneficiaries)
a.   General Adult
b.
c.

7. Requested Amount

Outright $ 51,000

Gift & Match $

NEH Total $ 51,000

Cost Sharing &
Other Contributions $

Total Project $ 51,000

Congressional
District   --

8. Field of Project
History & Crit. of Arts;
Women's Studies; Amer.
Social history

9. Location Where Project Will Be Completed

Texas, New York, California

10. Public Issues Of Project
The role of woman on the American stage

11. Topic (Title) of Project

MASKS & FACES

12. Description of Proposed Project (Do not exceed space provided)

Objectives: This is a request for development funds leading to a one-hour pilot script which explores our changing society through the eyes of American playwrights The history of American drama will serve as the vehicle for examining social attitudes, values, and thoughts. Program: The pilot show explores the changing image of woman as depicted on the American stage. A carefully selected montage of scenes will highlight the range of emerging ideas and values from the early days of American drama to contemporary times. Dramatic scenes will be interspersed with archival footage and photographs derived from that period of time. Our thematic link is the narrator, Helen Hayes, who will help place the scenes into cultural context. Personnel: The project directors have been active in commercial and public television as writers-producers (see attached Vitae). The Advisory Board is comprised of noted theatre historians, cultural historians, and others engaged in the study of societal issues (see attached Vitae).

13a. Have you submitted, or do you plan to submit a similar application to another NEH Program? If yes, provide name(s):[year(s) when applicable]

No

13b. Have you submitted, or do you plan to submit a similar application to another government or private entity? If yes, provide name(s): [year(s) when applicable]

No

IMPORTANT — READ INSTRUCTIONS CAREFULLY BEFORE COMPLETING BLOCKS 14 & 15

14. Authorizing Official (name & mailing address)

Spectrum IV Prods.
Austin, Texas 78702

Certification: I certify the statements herein are true and correct to the best of my knowledge and belief:

Sig. _____ Date   /   /
authorizing official/applicant   mo day yr

15. Institution/Organization (name & mailing address)

Spectrum IV Productions
Austin, Texas 78702

Type Ins./Org.:

• • •

Let's examine the Face Sheet to identify some terms and to answer some questions you may have about filling it out.

Item #1 asks for the name of the individual applicant or project director. In non-commercial television, the project director is equivalent to an executive producer. This is the person (or persons) responsible for creating the show and overseeing the total creative and administrative activities.

Item #2 asks whether the proposal is new or was submitted in some other form earlier. The application is considered *new* if it was never submitted to the agency before. It is a *revision* if it was submitted and was rejected previously. It is a *renewal* if it is based on work done in an earlier grant (e.g., a request for production based on a script development grant). A *supplemental* request is one that is an extension of current grant activities.

Item #3 asks the name of the "Program." This refers to the name of the division within the agency, as it appears on the program announcement.

Item #4 asks if the applicant is an individual or an organization. If you are applying as a freelance writer or independent producer, you would specify *individual*. If you are applying as a production entity or joint venture, you would check *institution,* and specify the type of company (e.g., Television Production) as well as private or non-profit status. Unless an agency specifically requests evidence of non-profit status in advance, you can generally incorporate *after* a grant is awarded.

Item #5 asks for the grant period, i.e., when the project will start and finish. As a rule, the start date should be several weeks *after* you expect to hear about the award decision. That assures you that your time won't be wasted waiting for a letter of confirmation, while the grant period is already in effect. Similarly, the completion date ought to provide you ample time to finish the project. It is not unusual for script development requests to be six months long. That length of time serves as a contingency since federal agencies are reluctant to authorize extensions later on.

Item #6 asks you to define the intended audience. You can take your cue from the stated objectives of the agency. One might be primarily interested in reaching general adult audiences; others might be targeted for minority, handicapped, bilingual, aged, children, etc.

Item #7 asks for the amount of funds required to accomplish the project. The money requested directly from the agency is called an *outright* grant. The *gifts & matching* category refers to money that might be forthcoming from other sources. Some agencies require a gifts & matching situation, i.e., they will offer money contingent upon your ability to raise a matching sum from another source. *Cost-sharing* refers to the contributions received in the form of service, facilities, and similar donations from your own production company.

Item #8 asks for the field of the project. This refers to the specific subject category as it relates to the agency's announcement (e.g., history of the theatre; women's studies; American studies).

Item #9 asks for the chief location in which most of the work will be accomplished during the grant period. It is a curious category for freelance writers, and can generally be listed as your home state. The purpose of this type of question is to provide the agency with a broad base of data to determine how effectively they serve their constituencies.

Item #10 asks for the public issues of the project. This refers to the thematic issues of relevance to the agency (e.g., "the role of woman on the American stage").

Item #11 asks for the Topic/Title. This is the complete working title of the project.

Item #12 asks for a description of the proposed project. This is an extremely important item, since it defines the objectives and approach in a paragraph or two. The synopsis should clearly and succinctly define the intentions, the filmic approach, the proposed content, and the key personnel involved. You'll be able to flesh out all that information later in the attached narrative proposal.

Writing The Narrative Proposal

The *Narrative* is the body of your request; it functions as a series presentation, fully detailing the concept and filmic approach of the show. The Narrative may run 20–100 pages or more, depending on the nature of the project. The narrative section expands upon the ideas proposed in the abstract. Objectives are clarified, approaches are defined, and sample visual treatments are provided. In a request for script development funds, a fully detailed pilot story or treatment is also included. If a production grant is sought, the full script is needed, and a budget breakdown is required.

A well-written narrative generally covers each of these areas in depth:
1) the nature and scope of the project;
2) the importance of the project to target audiences and general audiences;
3) the selected format and visual approach for television;
4) the timetable for research, development and/or production;
5) the background and expertise of key personnel;
6) the budget.

The narrative section is the heart of a grant proposal. Objectives should be stated clearly and the program content should be relevant to those goals. A treatment is particularly important, since it gives the reader a specific sense of the program you have in mind; it is the basis for determining *how* you intend to script the show. Treatments for public television are written precisely the same as those for commercial television.

The Budget

A budget is an integral part of a public television proposal. It demonstrates the creator's ability to plan accurately, realistically, and professionally. Moreover, it assures the funding agency that the money will be spent reasonably.

"But wait!" you say, "I'm a writer! What do I know about budgets!" That's a reasonable, plaintive cry. The fact is, in non-commercial television, the creator must be equipped to think like a *hyphenate* (writer-producer).

There is no model budget to examine, since individual projects differ considerably. However, certain elements do tend to appear regularly. For example, in script development the budget generally includes costs for scriptwriting, research, travel, consultant fees, typing and duplicating, administrative overhead, and so on. The actual cost for each item is dependent upon the development needs of a particular show.

This is not to suggest there are no budget guidelines for research and development. In fact, you can refer to the Writers' Guild of America *M. B. A.* (Minimum Basic Agreement) for public television rates for writing. The agreement reached between WGA and KCET-TV in Los Angeles provides some relevant guidelines. According to that agreement, minimums for writing an hour drama range from $10,378–$11,001. After 1981, the rates will be renegotiated upward. (Sample minimums from the WGA-KCET agreement appear on page 148 of this book.) Those fees are minimums for national airing over PBS. You may find that you require *more* money to develop a quality project aimed at national audiences.

Consultants are individual academic or technical advisors to the project. You may find that one or two will be sufficient for the project, or that a full-fledged 15-member Advisory Board is necessary. Usually consultants for public television receive an honorarium of $100–$300 per day. The number of days should be clarified in the budget; their role responsibilities should also be clarified in the narrative.

As for travel costs incurred in researching or developing a script, it's necessary to know who must travel where and for how long. Funding agencies will support travel, but the costs must be justified in the budget. Airplane trips should be coach fare, and *per diem* costs should be within standard federal guidelines. The funding agency, itself, can offer *per diem* guidelines for travel in both domestic and foreign cities.

Production budgets are much more difficult to determine than script costs. If you are seeking funds for production on the basis of a completed script it is essential to get some professional help. At the local public television level, a staff production manager can supply you with Rate Sheets, *i.e.*, the established costs for using station facilities and personnel. If the show is to be produced on a grander level, an independent producer or production manager can help break down costs for *above-the-line* (talent and creative staff) and *below-the-line* items (technical services and facilities).

The Directors Guild of America might help you locate specific people for the purpose of budgeting a show. In addition, other key guilds and unions can provide you with up-to-date information concerning going-rates. (Those guilds are listed in the *Appendix* of this book.) Make no mistake: production budgeting requires a professional and experienced hand.

How Projects Are Evaluated

Every agency has a different review system but the general process remains the same. PBS and CPB review projects in cooperation with each other and will try to find support and distribution for the projects of the highest merit. Regional groups of public television stations also review projects for development and prospective funding, *e.g.* SECA (Southern Educational Communication Association), and EEN (Eastern Educational Network). They assess the project's relevance to their membership stations and the potential for funding by outside sources.

Independent PBS stations also accept submissions. WNET-TV, New York, for example, evaluates each proposal submitted to the Program Planning Department. Their staff determines 1) if the proposal reflects priority needs of the station; 2) if the program is innovative and unique (*i.e.*, not duplicating other projects in work); 3) if funding potential exists. Once they approve the project, negotiations take place between the station and the creator.

Those agencies that have *RFP's* (requests for proposals) literally have a point system for ranking proposals. The various segments of the proposal are judged according to specified criteria in the guidelines. The proposal with the highest ranking receives the award.

One of the most sophisticated evaluation systems is set up by the

National Endowment for the Humanities. NEH puts the proposal through a rigorous review process. The staff selects scholars in appropriate fields and professionals in the television industry to comment on each proposal. Outside reviewers might literally include a Hollywood writer, a network executive, a studio production manager, a philosopher, an anthropologist, and an American cultural historian. While the reviewers send in their comments, a special media panel is convened. The panel consists of 10–15 people who represent a wide range of experience and interests in the industry and academic circles. The panel meets for two days—much like a sequestered jury—discussing each proposal on its own merits and in comparison with other projects submitted in that cycle.

The NEH staff forwards the recommendations of reviewers and panelists to the National Council on the Humanities. The Council is comprised of Presidential appointees who generally endorse the recommendations of reviewers, panelists, and staff. The Council recommends action to the Chairman of the Endowment, who has sole legislative authority to make final decisions about funding. Most often, those decisions are consistent with the advice received from the evaluation process.

The process sounds terribly cumbersome, but in fact the applicant gets a definitive word in 3–4 months from the submission deadline—a much faster turnaround time than at the networks. In addition, if you request the information, the staff will provide you with complete copies of the reviews, and a summary of the panelists' comments. To give you a sense of the batting average for successes, approximately one out of four projects will be recommended for funding.

The National Endowment for the Arts has a similar, though less complicated review process. The staff reviews the applications and refers them to appropriate advisory panels. The panel comments are reviewed by members of the National Council on the Arts, and they in turn recommend approval or disapproval to the Chairman of the Endowment. Once again, the Chairman has sole legislative authority to make final decisions, but will most often act on the advice and recommendations of the Council. The applicant is notified of acceptance or rejection by the Chairman's office.

What Happens If Your Project Is Funded?

If a project is funded, the creative rights in public television are usually retained by the writer or project director. However, the question of rights should be fully investigated—and negotiated—before the signing of any agreement. NEH, for example, gives the grantee total control over the project and total ownership of creative rights. As for profits, a new policy allows the first $50,000 in annual program income to go directly to the grantee (the writer or producer). Once a project earns more than $50,000 in any year, the excess is split 50%-50% with NEH, up to the amount of the original grant award. From that point on, all program income can be retained by the grantee. In some cases, the grantee can retain all program income for five years, provided that any excess over $50,000 is used for continuous development of humanities programs.

As for productions aimed at public broadcasting, the standard PBS agreement goes into effect (3 runs over a given period of time). Any other form of distribution—network syndicated, theatrical, secondary must be cleared with the funding agency. It's up to you to get complete information about a particular agency's stance on royalties, profits, and rights. If the policies seem carved in stone, there's probably no room for negotiation. However, if there *is* some latitude, it can't hurt to point to NEH's policy as a guideline to follow.

PART TWO

STORY AND CHARACTER DEVELOPMENT

5

Developing the Story
or Treatment

The Importance of Plot

Whether you write for the major networks or PBS, a dramatic presentation requires a solidly written story or treatment. It's the plot of the story that can make or break a show.

Dramatic critics have argued for centuries about the importance of plot. Aristotle called it the first and foremost principle in drama, the "soul" of tragedy. George Pierce Baker, the granddaddy of American playwriting teachers argued in *Dramatic Technique* that characters are of prime importance; their very presence affects others in the scene, and therefore the action in the scene is bound to be affected. The French critic, Ferdinand Bruntiere, in *The Law of the Drama* argued that drama is based on the conflict of wills among characters. In his excellent book, *The Art of Dramatic Writing*, Lajos Egri concurred that characters are of prime importance. And the arguments continue today with critics taking every possible side.

Obviously, it is difficult to separate plot from character in the well-developed treatment or script. However, the dictates of television almost require the predominance of plot as the "heart" of television drama or comedy. The television writer creates a story which inherently feeds on visual imagery to sustain viewer interest and appeal. If that appeal diminishes, or is absent, viewers can simply flip a dial to watch another program. The competitive and technological nature of the medium requires quick and effective plotting to sustain viewer interest.

As evidence of the heightened importance of plot, one might look at the basic conflict structure in most television drama. Generally, the conflict is external to the character, *i.e.*, he or she must overcome some obstacle imposed by others to achieve some goal. On the other hand, a character drama is based on inner decisions and conflicts. If those conflicts are not externalized into action, the story becomes static and talky, rather than dramatic, visual, and emotionally compelling.

This is not to imply that character development is not important in the well-crafted treatment or script. The character *must* be integrally related to the plotting, and *must* be credibly motivated and dimensionally conceived. Otherwise the audience won't be able to identify, won't believe the developing action, and won't care about the outcome of the story.

And what about the importance of theme in a television script? If it's too heavy or predominant, it will stick out like a sore thumb. (Incidentally, the industry uses "theme" to identify the premise of a show, not the intellectual concept. The studio reader provides a thumbnail sketch of a writer's story; that's the story's theme.) Sometimes a writer consciously and deliberately pushes a message. When that happens, the entertainment value is lost and the personal or ideological statement overshadows the story appeal. Theme material is most effectively handled when it springs naturally from the integration of plot, character, and action.

How to Develop the Story

1. Finding the "Hook"

A story idea can be derived from any personal experience or observation, any music, poetry, or book that moved you, a newspaper article that intrigued you, any source under the sun that sparked your imagination. However, the selection of the story idea must be more rational. First and foremost, it must have a hook—a unique premise that will grip the audience immediately. If the hook is strong, the story has a much better chance of eventually reaching the screen and touching the lives of millions of viewers.

Here are a few headlines that appeared in the papers. They are good examples of story hooks.

"FIERY METEOR NEARLY MISSES U.S."

"CAMPERS LOST IN UNSEASONABLE BLIZZARD"

"F.B.I. AGENTS KILL WRONG MAN IN MISTAKEN IDENTITY CHASE"

"SCIENTISTS BAFFLED BY PULSING BLOBS IN TEXAS"

"FANS ROBBED—BEFORE BUS GETS TO TRACK"

All the stories are true, and with some dramatic license each offers intriguing potential for story development. However, the premises are much too broad in this present form. Specific stories and conflicts need to be defined, lead characters need to be suggested, and particular points of view need to be established in the development process.

The first headline, for example, deals with a near catastrophe—a meteor slamming into the U.S. That story could be told from any number of vantage points. The first step in story development is to identify the approach, conflict, point of view, and character. For example, this might be one approach:

—An aging scientist discovers a fiery meteor is about to hit the U.S.—but no one believes him.

Now the story has a featured character who can evoke empathy. It has a point of view, told from the perspective of an aging scientist. It has a built-in dramatic conflict with a "time-bomb" situation (the scientist must find a way to convince others—and to act—before the meteor strikes). As the story develops, other characters and sub-plots might be incorporated, but the basic premise is fairly well defined at the outset, and the hook can be told in a nutshell (or in a *TV Guide* blurb).

Look at the second story idea ("CAMPERS LOST IN UN-SEASONABLE BLIZZARD"), and try to define the best dramatic angle. You might choose the point of view of one camper or a number of them; or you might want to tell the story from the point of view of the rescuers. The basic conflict and plot pattern centers around a jeopardy situation, but *who* is in jeopardy, and how great is the sense of urgency for escape and survival? Those decisions dictate the direction and visual approach of the story.

2. Identifying Plot Patterns

Once you have an idea, it might be helpful to categorize the plot according to genre and situation. An early analysis of genre and plot patterns can help you keep a better handle on the story development.

If the story was meant to be dramatic but comedy elements come into play, the plot might be enriched by the interweaving of genres. However, once the comedy elements become dominant, the original intent is lost, and a different story is in the making.

The industry defines program types according to those listed by the Nielsen ratings company: general drama, suspense and mystery, situation comedy (or character comedy), Western drama, variety, feature films (which means theatrical motion pictures, not films made for television), informational programs, quiz and audience participation, children's programs, and sports events.

Dramatic critics and writers identify plot patterns from a more contextual standpoint. Georges Polti compiled a catalogue of "Thirty Six Dramatic Situations," which identifies basic plot patterns that appear in all dramatic stories. Lewis Herman, in *A Practical Manual of Screenplay Writing for Theatre and Television Films* reduced those patterns to nine: 1) *Love*—boy-meets-girl, loses-girl, wins-her-back-again; 2) *Success*—the lead character wants to achieve and succeed at all costs; 3) *Cinderella*—an "ugly duckling" is changed into a perfect human being; 4) *Triangle*—three characters are in a romantic entanglement; 5) *Return*—a long-lost lover, wandering father, missing husband returns; 6) *Vengeance*—a character seeks revenge for some wrong-doing (this is the basic pattern for suspense and mystery shows); 7) *Conversion*—the bad guy turns good; 8) *Sacrifice*—the lead character sacrifices his or her own good to help someone else; 9) *Family*—this pattern focuses on the interrelationship of characters in a single place and situation (on a plane, in a hotel, in a prison, on a farm). We might also add a tenth plot pattern, which is a favorite formula of the networks: 10) *Jeopardy*—a life and death situation, dealing with the survival instincts and prowess of the lead characters.

Plot patterns are not mutually exclusive, and any number of subplots can emerge within a given story. Still, this type of cataloguing provides the writer with a clearer overview of the dominant story elements, and the concurrent identification of background material. Once the dominant pattern is identified, there's a lesser chance of the writer being side-tracked by intriguing sub-plots or minor characters.

3. The Step Outline and Dramatic Action Points

One of the first problems in developing a story is knowing where to begin, i.e., establishing a *point-of-attack*. Why is this day, this moment, this situation *critical* to the lives of the leading characters? If the situation has great personal meaning for the characters, and helps establish the emerging plot, you'll have a much better chance of holding the audience throughout the progression of the story.

A common technique for plotting the progression of the story is a *Step Outline*, i.e., a condensed scene-by-scene version of the narrative action. Careful selection and placement of sequences can heighten the storytelling effect, and makes it much easier to move directly into script form. The question is, how do you select the most effective combination of scenes? Which scenes go where? Which characters are needed at what points? Which scenes build the conflict? Which scenes are extraneous?

Aristotle talked about the importance of the proper arrangement of incidents in a plot to have the greatest impact on the audience. Twentieth century critics still agree. Elder Olson, in *Tragedy and the Theory of Drama,* argued that story elements should be selected by a writer only to heighten dramatic credibility and the emotional impact on an audience. Similarly, Eric Bentley, in *Life of the Drama,* contended that a carefully arranged sequence of action is essential for achieving maximum effect. He called it a "rearrangement" of incidents as opposed to a simple chronological arrangement. In short, *dramatic* action rather than literal action.

I've found that the use of *dramatic action points* is an effective way to select and arrange key incidents in the story. I call them dramatic action points in deference to Aristotle's concept of a forward thrust in drama. These are the basic dramatic units and events which advance the story. Once action points are identified, they can be placed in different contexts (much like the restructuring of a puzzle) to strengthen the plot structure. They can be used to orchestrate the pacing and balance in the story.

The use of dramatic action points is an on-going process in the story development phase. As an example of how it might work, let's look at one of the premises mentioned earlier in the headlines:

"CAMPERS LOST IN UNSEASONABLE BLIZZARD"

We might try to outline these points for the opening sequences:

1. A family is en route to the Berkshires for a camping weekend.

2. They arrive and find the campgrounds in disarray, but decide
   to stay.

3. They get snowed in.

Even in this sketchy form, it becomes apparent that the point-of-attack is not strong. There is no suggestion of conflict or character. The action points can be revised accordingly:

1. A couple's marriage is shaky. The husband works too hard
    and they need a vacation.

2. They head up to the Berkshires for a camping weekend. He
    brought along work, anyway, and they argue.

3. They arrive at the campground, which is in disarray. It's
    late at night, and they decide to stay.

4. It snows.

But even here there are some problems. The points are too choppy,
and are not really comprised of individual dramatic sequences. The action needs to be clarified and the characters need more definition. It
might be possible to merge the first two action points for the sake of
pacing and add other people to the story—their children, other campers, perhaps even a pet that is lost in the storm.

This is what the revised outline might look like:

1. BARRY, SHARON, and KIDS ride to the campsite. We learn
    they have marriage problems.

2. They arrive at the campgrounds and find it in disarray.
    It's late, they're tired, they decide to stay.

3. Setting up camp, we meet other campers, and follow-up
    marriage conflict.

4. It snows as they sleep.

5. An expensive trailer reaches camp, finds no power. The
    irate owner blames Barry.

6. In morning, Barry's kids play in the snow. Their dog
    gets swept away in the river.

And so on. Dramatic action points provide a very bare—but specific—
blueprint for the structure of the story. There are roughly 21–26 major
action points in a 90-minute film, which translates to four or five pages
for each sequence in the script. Those are, of course, very general figures, but they do provide some guidance in assessing the time count for
an eventual script.

Here's how the action points might eventually translate into the treatment itself. The following Act is derived from these action points outlined above.

THE WIND CHILL FACTOR

April. A bright, spring day.

We follow BARRY and SHARON RUTLEDGE, and their SON

and DAUGHTER, riding in a new, but small camper

from New York City to the Berkshire Mountains.

Throughout the trip, we hear innocuous commentary

from the radio about a cold front moving in from

Canada. But the noise is lost in the sounds of

the children at play, and the dog barking.

This derives from Action Point # 1

The marriage is rocky. BARRY is a lawyer who

works too hard and is constantly afraid he won't

be advanced. This family weekend was arranged to

save the marriage; but BARRY has brought along a

legal brief, anyway.

They reach the Berkshires just at dusk, and follow

the signs to the campground. They drive down a

steep dirt road, into a valley nestled among the

mountains. But when they arrive, they find the

campgrounds in disarray. A sign that reads "OFFICE"

points to some prefabricated walls lying unassembled

Action point # 2

on the ground. Another car is parked nearby--a VW. The young couple inside, STEPHEN and MARIAN, commiserate with the RUTLEDGE's; they, too, made reservations, but the campground obviously went bankrupt before it could open.

They're all undecided about what to do. They should find another campground. But it's getting dark, and there's a storm brewing. Besides, this place can shelter them--the campsites are cleared, there are picnic tables, fireplaces, there's a centrally-located water pipe, and there are two outhouses, one male, one female. The two couples decide to stay until morning, when the storm will be over.

Action
point
3

BARRY struggles through the unfamiliar tasks of setting up a campsite, and he is forced to finish in the rain. Thunder and lightning follow him as he returns to the camper, drenched to the bone. The KIDS think it's outrageously funny.

Another car arrives, drawn by the light from the lanterns. It's a group of HIPPIES, two boys and a girl, who set up a rudimentary tent in a nearby campsite.

Inside the RUTLEDGE camper, after dinner, the family goes to bed, accompanied by the sound of rain on the roof. SHARON bickers with BARRY, who refuses to go to bed without reading over his brief. Angry, SHARON gets into bed. BARRY reads. The sound of the rain peters out. BARRY offers his wife some minimal consolation--at least it's stopped raining.

Action point #4

But in a WIDE SHOT of the campground, we see that it's begun snowing.

****

Action point #5

During the night, a sleek, flashy, expensive-looking silver trailer arrives in the snow, driven by CHARLES EVANS who is camping with his wife, MAGGIE, and their teenage daughter, BETH. The family is dismayed to see the condition of the campground, and an irate CHARLES follows the only visible light--BARRY's--to register his complaint.

BARRY is surprised to see it snowing, but he suggests that CHARLES do what everyone else has done; camp here for the night. After all, how long can a snowstorm last in April?

CHARLES tries to connect his electrical system to the power outlet at the campsite, but finds that the power has not been turned on. He's furious; now he has no heat. And, like everyone else, he has no cold-weather clothing. Disgruntled, he bundles up his family into the silver trailer for the night. Gradually, the campground light go out, first in the EVANS camper, then in BARRY's.

Action point #6

In the morning, it is still snowing heavily. The RUTLEDGE KIDS, eager to build a springtime snowman, find make-shift winter clothing--dishrags for their ears, pinned-up blankets for sweaters, plastic bags for galoshes. And they rush out into the snow, with their dog, to play.

When SHARON calls them to breakfast, the dog

(a city dog, used to a leash) bolts and races

along the edge of a small river. The pup loses

its footing in the snow, falls into the water,

and is swept downstream.

This is all
derived
from
Action
point
6

The KIDS race along the riverbank, following

their pet, plodding through the snow, calling

to him. STEPHEN spots them, races over, and

restrains them from following the dog. He tries

to explain they can't save their pet. It couldn't

see the footing in the snow; neither can they.

But the children are unheeding; they scream and

cry as they watch their pet sweep out of sight...

****

4. Plotting Audience Interest

It helps to visualize the plot in terms of a graph which measures intended audience interest. Many television programs literally go through the process of audience testing to provide studios and networks with some idea of the program's effectiveness. By means of electronic testing, a graph is generated and instantaneous viewer response is recorded. Producers can literally see how every joke, line, car chase, action sequence, or romantic intrigue holds audience interest. Writers can apply that same principle to the plotting of the story; they can creatively "manipulate" audience interest levels.

For example, a two-hour television film might be charted as follows:

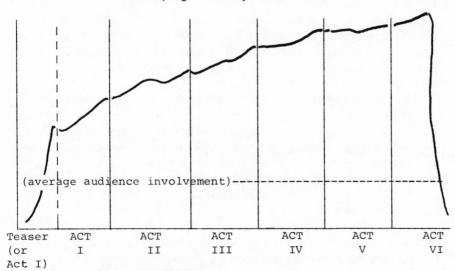

(average audience involvement) --

Teaser	ACT	ACT	ACT	ACT	ACT	ACT
(or	I	II	III	IV	V	VI
Act I)						

If you read from left to right, you can see that the short teaser was very effective as a hook, and that each act break was designed to maximize audience interest up until the commercial breaks. Interest picks up, with a snowballing effect throughout the entire show, and sustains until the end of Act VI.

If we were dealing with motion pictures, the chart might look a little different. The writer has more time to develop characters and can build a slower pace that increases throughout the film. The result is a skewed bell-shaped curve:

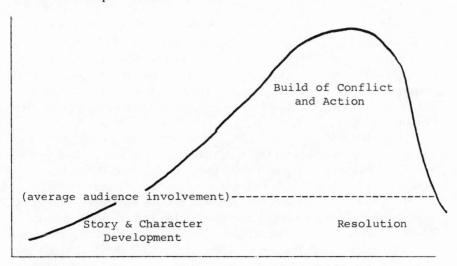

Build of Conflict and Action

(average audience involvement) --------------------------------

Story & Character Development

Resolution

(No Act Breaks in Feature Films)

The plot interest curve, or audience interest curve, is just one more conceptual device to help visualize the story in development. It helps set the pacing of the story as it unfolds, and suggests the intensity of action sequences and dramatic interrelationshps that can sustain—and build—audience interest.

The treatment serves as the foundation for the entire script. With the right amount of visualization, character development, suspense builds, and comedy relief, the reader will get an accurate picture of the show. Conceptual devices for story development can help sharpen that impact and appeal.

Adaptations

With an increased marketplace for TV films based on previously published stories, the process of adapting literary works for televison has become an important concern for many writers. In the novel or short story, an author can spend a great deal of time on character development, exposition, the free association of time and place, and so on. The reader can pick up the pages at any time, read or reread any segment at will. In television, that same story must be told in a 90-minute or 120-minute structure. That means streamlining the plot and characters. The writer must be an artistic surgeon, with a very fine and sensitive touch, knowing what must go and what must stay. Ideally, the television adaptation should remain faithful to the original work, conveying the same feeling, atmosphere, plot, and characterization—even though scenes, characters, and conflicts have been modified.

As for new writers adapting published works, it will be no more than an exercise if exclusive rights for televison and film are not obtained in advance. Producers, networks, and studios are in a constant competitive bidding situation for new material and they have enormous financial resources behind them. Chances are very slim that they'll miss a newly published piece, and even slimmer that a newcomer will outbid them.

With that discouraging reality, a determined writer might still dig up an old paperback from the attic that has outstanding visual potential, or a magazine story in a local publication, or a second-hand account of an incident that has earmarks of an exciting television film.

If you do find a project that seems suited for television adaptation, investigate the copyright situation thoroughly before blocking out the filmic approach. Contact the publisher, or the attorney for the estate, to be certain that the rights are available. If you're lucky, you might get the rights for a percentage of profits. Then, again, you might have to pay for it dearly.

The actual form of adapted works is precisely the same as an original treatment, although it must convey the appropriate atmosphere, characterization, and dramatic integrity of the published novel or story. The use of dramatic action points and audience interest curves can help define the best plotting structure.

On the following pages you'll find the opening segment from a fifty page treatment, "The Watchmaker," based on the book, *A Teaspoon of Honey*. Although you may not be familiar with the book, you might still sense the character orientation of the original piece and the integrity of the adaptation to a specific style. In this particular format—which is both narrative and visual—the scene identification headings are kept to an absolute minimum.

FADE IN.

Sochi, Russia - 1902.

A brisk autumn air blows through the open door of the Malinsky Brothers Watch Shop, as HERSCHEL MALINSKY, 20 years old, impatiently straightens the magnifying loupe over his eye. Outside the shop, the boardwalk is almost deserted; the lodges on the hillside are virtually empty. His older brother JACOB glances up from his work, almost reading his thoughts. "It would be nice if you were here when the tourists come again." HERSCHEL nods. He'll try not to think of his impending term in the army, or how the Czar's soldiers declare free reign on Jews. "At least I'll get to see momma and poppa in Schershov before I leave." JACOB will worry about his brother, even though HERSCHEL seems blessed with the survival instinct...He survived near death as an infant, so weak on the day of his circumcision...He outwitted AUNTIE TAUBE, who tried to enslave him and humiliate him when he lived there as a teenager...He emerged safe from the massacre of the Jews in Kishenev last year...And now he'll be a Jewish soldier in the Russian Army. With God's help, he'll survive that, too.

HERSCHEL and his friend LEE are celebrating his last few weeks
in Sochi. They're on a forest trail, warmed by a pitcher of
vodka, lying sprawled out in the grass. A tin of tobacco lies
nearby, a gift from LEE, a gentile friend who treats him like a
brother. This is the way it should be...And then, wobbling to
his horse, he responds to a challenge: "Let's race!" HERSCHEL
climbs into the saddle, breaks into a grin, and takes off. LEE's
horse falls behind, HERSCHEL's horse sprints ahead. But soon the
animal stumbles, throwing its rider helplessly to the ground.
LEE dismounts quickly and rushes to his friend's aid. HERSCHEL
sits himself up, and feels for any broken bones. Instead, he
finds a ragged piece of cloth hanging from his trouser leg. "I
tore my pants!" LEE laughs, "You're lucky that's all you tore."
HERSCHEL bemoans his fate; his tailor is out of town. But LEE
has heard of a seamstress on Minskovoy Street. She just moved into
the area. "A seamstress!" HERSCHEL looks as if he'll fall from
his horse again. "I need a suit mended, not a petticoat hemmed!"
LEE smiles, "Maybe she'll mend your knee with satin, my friend?"

On Minskovoy Street, LEE rides the horses back to the stable as
HERSCHEL, newly changed, stands in front of a brown cottage, his
trousers slung over his shoulder like a shawl. Feeling uncomfort-
able, he knocks. He's certainly in no mood for this kind of thing.
A man should not have to rely on a woman to fix his pants. Besides,
the woman is probably an old hag...The door opens, and we see
HERSCHEL's P.O.V. -- MIRIAM stands before him, an astonishing
looking eighteen year old girl, red hair piled high on her head,
eyes green and wide. After a beat, she moves back into the house,
replaced by MR. PELTZMAN, a smallish man with a yarmulke on his
head, a prayer book in his hand. He looks quizzically at HERSCHEL,
who seems immobilized. Finally, HERSCHEL holds out the pants
in his hand and stumbles out the words: "Is this the dress-

maker's...?" The man ushers him in and introduces him to his
daughter MIRIAM. She watches, from the front of the fireplace,
stroking her cat, smiling slowly. "I think I'll stay until these
are mended," HERSCHEL says.

The next night, as crazy as it seems, HERSCHEL scrambles through
his dresser drawers, finding a shirt which needs mending. JACOB,
watching from the bed, sees his brother pop off a shirt button and
lay it aside. After the expected inquiry, HERSCHEL explains too
casually that the seamstress can work wonders. Besides, since
when can't a grown man have his clothes repaired if he wants.
JACOB shrugs knowingly.

HERSCHEL is like a new man with a new life blood. In his watch
shop, he works diligently and happily until a customer happens
to mention that a marriage is being arranged between SCHMUEL
RAZNIKOFF and that new seamstress in town. But he's heard that
the dowry isn't enough. Good gossip, isn't it?

That night, HERSCHEL bolsters himself, and heads back to the
PELTZMAN house with a shirt held tight in hand. He knocks on the
door of the brown cottage, and MR. PELTZMAN greets him. With
the door open, HERSCHEL can see SCHMUEL RAZNIKOFF on the sofa
beside MIRIAM. He drops his shirt to the floor and MR. PELTZMAN
picks it up. Seeing MIRIAM's imploring face, he says, "Nu,
Herschel? You come every night with something to be mended. The
others bring only themselves. If you'll come by tomorrow, Miriam
will see you at 8:00 by yourself." An open-mouthed HERSCHEL
stumbles out, "Thank you..."

HERSCHEL manages to see MIRIAM for two weeks, in the synagogue
and in the house, but always MR. PELTZMAN sits with the Talmud in

hand, not leaving them alone. Maybe tonight will be different.
It's his last night in Sochi. As he walks to the brown cottage
on Minskovoy Street, he turns up the collar of his warm raincoat;
it's cold outside, it's drizzling. He silently curses the army
as he looks up at MIRIAM's house. The lights are on. He tries
to see.if MR. PELTZMAN is in his customary chair, but he can't
make out the figures in the window. He knocks. MIRIAM answers
the door, dressed beautifully in a long, full dress with white
lace. He would love to sweep her into his arms, but he can only
follow her to the warm fire inside. MR. PELTZMAN closes his prayer
book and rises awkwardly, excusing himself for a glass of tea.
They're alone! The fire crackles in the fireplace, the rain splat-
ters against the windows, and HERSCHEL can only fumble with his
cigarette papers and tobacco. MIRIAM sits close beside him, and
they talk quietly. Then HERSCHEL touches her face and slowly
presses his lips to hers. She responds hesitantly at first, then
kisses him with erratic passion. She draws away now, lifts her
hand, and slaps him hard across the cheek: "You shouldn't kiss
me like that, Herschel. No girl should be kissed like that except
by her husband." "I want to be your husband," he says. "Let's
ask your poppa." MIRIAM responds warmly, but MR. PELTZMAN is
already shuffling back into the room. "You think I should let my
daughter sit until her curls turn gray?" HERSCHEL rises. "After
the army, we'll have the rest of our lives together." HERSCHEL
and MIRIAM look expectantly toward the old man, who adjusts the
yarmulke on his head. The silence seems to last forever. "Herschel,
already I like you. Come back on furlough and we can talk then."
HERSCHEL breaks into a smile and shakes his hand. "A chance is
all I ask." And now he turns to MIRIAM, addressing her quietly.
"Just wait for me. I'll be back for you, I promise."

At his apartment, he undresses quietly, trying not to wake JACOB. But JACOB was hardly asleep, worrying about his brother's trip in the morning. HERSCHEL packs his things carefully -- MIRIAM's gift of cakes, LEE's gift of tobaccos, and all the things he bought for his family: the gray wool shawl for MOMMA; the heavy union suit for POPPA; the scarf for ESTHER. And now he carefully packs his watchmaking tools, wrapped in a piece of flannel cloth. JACOB watches his brother sadly. "You'll send my love to momma and poppa and Esther?" His younger brother nods dutifully. "And, Herschel," JACOB continues, "You'll take care in the army?"

HERSCHEL turns to him with a forced smile. "Don't worry, Jacob. I'll take such care, they'll make me a Captain." JACOB frowns. "A Jew a Captain? Never! You'd make jokes at your own funeral." HERSCHEL finishes packing in the darkness.

MIRIAM sits quietly by the fire, trying to concentrate on her sewing. But all she can think about is HERSCHEL MALINSKY. No man has ever stirred her the way HERSCHEL has. She puts down her sewing, crosses to her father who is busy reading in his chair. She leans over and kisses his forehead, thanking him. If any man is worth waiting for, HERSCHEL is that man. She goes back to the fire and prays silently for his safekeeping and quick return.

• • •

As you can see, the form of this adaptation is the same as any treatment. What you may notice is that the opening sequences seem to emphasize character development and interrelationships, rather than the traditional action or "tease" emphasis of episodic TV. Since this adaptation is for a two-part film (4 hours), it is structured more like a film epic than a television episode. As a result, it's possible to *slowly* develop the characters and build toward the conflicts and tensions that will hold an audience throughout the multi-part story.

6

Developing the Character and Dialogue

Character Development and "The Method" Writer

Characters move a story forward through credible motivations, actions, reactions, and interrelationships. They must be totally identifiable—whether good, bad, or indifferent. They must be real people, with a consistent pattern of behavior, and a complete psycho-social-physical frame-of-reference.

It may be difficult to develop the complex innuendoes of character in the treatment stage where dialogue is limited. Nonetheless, the writer can paint intricate portraits of the character through behavioral action and reaction. Let's take, for example, the character of a boss who can no longer employ his secretary; he is impelled to find her another job. If the literal route is taken, the scene opens in his office where the two confront each other, and he picks up the phone to find her work. That literal approach waters down the potential of the character and the depth of intentions and attitudes. It would be more effective if the audience sees the boss alone, clearly upset at the impending task. When the secretary comes in, he puts on a supervisory air, informs her that she's fired. The secretary may resist, fight, or storm out in anger, but the boss remains resolute, maintaining his composure throughout the ordeal. Only after she leaves does he let down his defenses. He can take a *Beat* (a "Beat" is a dramatic moment in which the character makes internal transitions in thought or attitude). Then he picks up the phone, calls a colleague, and recommends a damn good employee. That action, in the privacy of his office, makes him a more sympathetic character in the eyes of the audience. He's not out to gain anything or prove anything. He's acting in the best interests of a sacrifice pattern.

Such private moments are very important for establishing the true inner nature of characters. The audience can see how genuinely concerned they are, how brutal, how comic, how gentle, how disturbed. It helps to build in a sense of vulnerability or susceptibility for each character. That makes them more identifiable and provides a more interesting dimension to their behavior. Even the traditional bad guy should be justifiably motivated. Perhaps he's driven by anguish, frustration, deprivation, jealousy. The audience can understand that kind of motivation, although the action might not be condoned.

Knowing the character's inner life is a crucial part of story development and scripting. You might not be able to define inner realities at the conceptual stage, but in the process of development, the character's personality emerges. The writer must know who the character is, how the character thinks, reacts, interrelates, behaves in any given situation. One of the best ways to accomplish this is through an analytical technique similar to *The Method* approach used by actors trained in a modified American version of the Stanislavski system of acting. Constantin Stanislavski was a Russian director whose acting principles reshaped the twentieth century stage; he provided new "tools" for achieving realism.*

The Method actor approaches his or her craft with a disciplined sense of creativity and spontaneity. In this sense, "disciplined" means using the tools at one's disposal to create a sense of inner life for the characters in every scene of the script, from beginning to end. *The Method* writer can flesh out the text and sub-text in every scene. He or she is sensitive to the motivations of characters, the consistency of attitudes, the justifiable actions and reactions in the plot structure. The writer gets to play every part, and if a behavioral problem is discovered, there's still time to fix it in a rewrite.

Here are some of the analytical questions a *Method* writer might ask to keep a firm hold on the behavioral realities in story and character development:

---

*The Stanislavski system of acting was adapted by Lee Strasberg, among others, at the Group Theatre in New York in the 1930's. Strasberg put new emphasis on inner technique and psychological realism, which became the cornerstone for training at the Actors Studio. That interpretation of Stanislavski's work became known as *The Method,* and was at the heart of artistic controversy in the 1950's. It remains the staple for acting realism in film, TV, and theatre today. For more on *The Method,* see *Annotated Bibliography* at the back of this book.

1) *What is the Super-Objective of the Story?*

The "super-objective" is the writer's main purpose for developing a story. The aim may be to build suspense, offer new insights, make an audience laugh, grip them in terror. When you define that objective it's easier to gauge the effectiveness of character development, visual action, dramatic mood, plot sequences, and filmic pacing.

2) *What is the Through-Line-of-Action for Each Character?*

The "through-line-of-action" is a conceptual thread which shows how each character fits into your main objective. Each character serves a very specific function in relation to the plot development and the realization of your thematic goals. Each scene should bring you closer to those goals.

3) *What is the Character's Intention?*

The "intention" is a character's planned action. It can usually be stated as an infinitive—to relax, to rob a bank, to go shopping, to keep a secret, etc. A character's intention may change from scene to scene, and may even change within the scene itself (given the properly motivated transitions).

4) *What is the Character's Motivation?*

The "motivation" explains *why* a character wants to achieve a specific intention. It is the *inner need* for the action. For example, if a character wants to leave her husband, there might be any number of emotional factors contributing to that decision. However, one motivation may be dominant: she may be in love with someone else; she may be frustrated, unfulfilled, afraid, bored. The motivation imprints a uniqueness to the character, and provides a psychological framework for action and reaction throughout the treatment and script.

5) *What is the Character's Sense of Urgency?*

A "sense of urgency" tells the viewer how *badly* your character wants to fulfill his or her intention. A rule of thumb here: *the greater the sense of urgency, the greater the dramatic conflict.* The character needs to adjust, adapt, or overcome the situation to achieve a state of harmony (or to achieve consonance).

6) *What is the Character's State of Being?*

The "state of being" is a character's total psychological and physical frame of reference in a scene. A writer creates more realistic dimensions by incorporating given circumstances into the character's thoughts, behavior, and attitudes. Let's create a scene with these given circumstances as an example. Steve is frantic to see Marian. He runs over to her apartment and finds it empty. It's been raining, it's late at night. What behavioral reality needs to be conveyed? Steve is wet, cold, out of breath, concerned, anguished. The writer may have to convey all that without a line of dialogue. The stage directions might suggest this: *"Steve slams open the door, glances anxiously around the room, sees no one. Breathing hard, he wipes the rain from his face."* And so the stage directions can paint reality through description, keeping alive all the elements in the given circumstances of the scene.

7) *Are the Moment-to-Moment Realities Established in the Scene?*

The "moment-to-moment" reality is a character's reaction to each and every dramatic unit in the scene. A character needs ample time to build attitudes and to shift thoughts in order to be credible to an audience. Once again, let's create a scene to show how the concept works.

Suppose we're in Berta's apartment when a power failure hits Los Angeles. When the lights go out, she would never think the whole city is powerless. She would have to build logically to that moment of discovery. First, she might try the light switch, or test the bulb in a lamp. Then she might discover that the light is out in the next room. She might search for a flashlight to take to the fusebox. And that's where she discovers that the apartment building went dark. She still has no idea of the scope of the blackout. She goes out into the street and finds the whole block is out. And then, through a neighbor, she learns the momentous reality—the whole city is dark.

Meanwhile, what are her moment-to-moment *attitudes*? This depends on Berta's state of being, her intention in the scene when it opened, her motivations and sense of urgency. If she were dressing for an important night out, the power loss would be frustrating, but she would go through each moment credibly to *build* that frustration. At first, she would simply be annoyed. That motivates her to correct the situation by finding another light bulb. However, the power is out in the other room. Her reaction? Greater annoyance. She can't complete her intention. Now she learns the whole apartment building is dark. Her attitude: Frustration! She'll *never* be able to get ready on time. When she learns the whole city is dark, her attitude is coupled with anxiety and curiosity. Each moment can be played out credibly, and each reaction conveyed effectively to the viewer. With the proper builds and reactions, the writer can avoid inconsistent or "manipulated" action which forces an incident or telegraphs the story. A viewer may know the lights went out in L.A., but there is no way for the character to know it until she experiences the actual moment of discovery.

That same moment-to-moment technique can be used for building tensions in a scene. Suppose an escaped convict is hiding in the closet of Berta's room. The viewers may know the danger, but Berta doesn't. You can play up those realities in the story, and orchestrate the pacing of the drama. Once the audience knows that danger lurks in the closet, you can take your time bringing Berta to that confrontation scene—and heighten suspense in the process. She may come inside the room, take off her coat, and head to the closet—then spot a newspaper on the table. She tosses her coat on the chair, glances at the paper, reads about the convict at large, and instinctively locks her front door. Now she heads to the closet with her coat—and the phone rings. She answers, but no one is on the line. She hangs up, reaches for a cigarette, and goes to the closet once more. This time she opens it, and—*nothing.* She gets a hanger, puts her coat away and turns to go. Then, suddenly, a hand reaches out, and *grabs* her—

You can play all those realities in the plot to heighten the eventual confrontation. Hold the audience, surprise them, play out all the moment-to-moment tensions. But now the story needs a *twist* (i.e., a surprise element in the plotline) to help Berta escape. Perhaps she breaks away through some ingenious action or special skill. If she has some special skill, it should be *planted* earlier in the story, so it won't appear to be contrived. A story *plant* provides a logical and proper build-up for action on the screen.

A good suspense story is usually brimming with unusual twists—sudden switches in the plot, "red herrings," the unexpected. If a character gets into a hopeless situation, and the audience is totally caught up in the action, it would be absolutely anticlimactic for the police to burst in suddenly and save her. The audience has seen that a hundred times before; the action becomes predictable and cliche.

One of the most useful devices for finding innovative twists is the *"What if—"* technique. As the story develops, ask a steady stream of *"What if—"* questions, until you find a number of different possibilities. "What if this happens? What would she do?" Try to go beyond the first immediate response. Give yourself a number of alternatives; try any combination of thoughts that are consistent with the credibility of the piece. The more you ask, *"What if—"*, the greater the possibility of keeping the story and characters alive and interesting. The reverse was aptly illustrated by a cartoon I remember seeing. A frustrated TV writer sits by his typewriter, completed pages strewn all over the room. The caption went something like this: "Oh, to hell with it! 'Suddenly a lot of shots rang out, and everyone fell dead. The End.' "

Dialogue: Problems and Solutions

Dialogue is an integral part of scripting, and is intricately bound up with character development. Inner values and motivations are communicated by the uniqueness of dialogue. What a character says—or doesn't say—tells us about that character's state of being.

Ideally, dialogue should be motivated by the given circumstances in the scene, and should be consistent with the character development already established. Just as the writer has an "inner eye" for visualization, he or she must have an "inner ear" for dialogue that makes the character come to life, adding a dimension of spontaneity and realism to the roles.

Sometimes writers have difficulty with dialogue. Lines may tend to be choppy, staccato, unrealistic, or, perhaps over-theatricalized. The script might be peopled with characters transposed from an English drawing room comedy ("quite grammatically correct, but evuh so boring, dahling"), or with characters misplaced from a 1950's version of *A Streetcar Named Desire* ("Well . . . uh . . . I . . . um . . . uh . . . well, y'know what I mean, huh? Don'cha? Hmm. . . ?).

To help identify and overcome those problems, here is a list of *The Ten Most Common Dialogue Problems and Solutions.*

1. Too Head-On

This is dialogue that is much too literal and embarrasingly obvious. It sounds very contrived. For example:

MARIAN comes in the door and STEVE smiles.

> STEVE
> Marian, I'm so glad to see
> you. I love you so much.
> I've been waiting to see you
> for so long.

That kind of dialogue is pretty embarrassing. No subtlety at all. It would be more effective if he were too overtaken to speak. Or, he might grab her close and say nothing. Then, after a *Beat,* he might say:

> STEVE
> Y'know, I can't stand to
> see you.

And they hug.

Well, of course, actions speak louder than words, and you've built a nice counter-point to the action. Marian knows what he means, and so does the audience. Subtlety can be achieved through understatement, "playing against" the expected material, and playing out the character sub-texts and inner attitudes.

2. Too Choppy

This is dialogue that is staccato. Filled with one liners. A word or two. When you thumb through the script it looks like a Pinter play rather than a realistic and cinematic vehicle. This is an example of dialogue that is too choppy:

```
                    MARSHALL
          I'm hungry.

                    SANDY
          Me too.

                    MARSHALL
          Let's go out to eat.

                    SANDY
          O.k.

                    MARSHALL
          Is the deli o.k.?

                    SANDY
          Yes, it's o.k.
```

One solution to the problem is providing credible motivation for dialogue. The characters need a motivation and intention for speaking. They need a pre-established pattern of thought and behavior. Marshall, for example, might be checking out the refrigerator through an earlier piece of action, then:

```
                    MARSHALL
          Hey, there's nothing in the
          fridge. Wanna go out for a
          bite?

                    SANDY
          Mmm.  I'm famished.
```

> MARSHALL
> How does the deli sound?
>
> SANDY
> Like chicken soup in heaven.

And they get ready to go.

In essence, the dialogue is the building block for moment-to-moment realities in the scene. It should spark behavioral action and reaction to be most effective.

3. Too Repetitious

Dialogue becomes repetitious when a character repeats himself or herself in a number of different ways. The character offers redundant information, or repetitive phrases:

> RONNIE
> I had such a good time on the trip. It was one of the best trips I ever had.
>
> ARNIE
> I'm glad you enjoyed the trip.
>
> RONNIE
> It was so good to be away. It was a terrific trip.

If the problem of repetition is examined, it might stem from one or two problems: the writer doesn't know what the character should say next, so relies on earlier dialogue; the writer is afraid the audience won't "get" a specific point unless the character emphasizes it in dialogue. One solution to redundancy in dialogue is to go back into the script and clearly motivate each speech—or delete the speech altogether. This is how the dialogue above might be handled in revision:

> ARNIE
> You must have had some time. I never saw you so excited about anything.
>
> RONNIE
> It was fantastic. I'm just sorry it's over.

The simple character interchange affects the whole point of the dialogue exchange. One character is reacting to the other's emotional and physical state-of-being in the scene.

As for points the viewer should get, it's helpful to put in some preliminary plants in the scene. Then a casual line of dialogue by a character is sufficient to trigger the "Aha!"-syndrome for the audience.

4. Too Long

Dialogue that is too long reads like an editorial speech or a philosophical diatribe. It creates static action in the script and often includes related problems of redundancy and preachiness. Let's examine this speech:

```
                    RITA
                  (to Anne)
        They fired you because you're
        a woman, not for any other reason.
        If you were a man you would have
        been promoted. Don't let them do
        that to you. Go back and fight for
        what you believe in. They wouldn't
        get away with that on me, I can
        assure you that. I remember when
        I was growing up, my mother always
        told me to look out for bigots
        like that. You've got to stand up
        and let them know you're not going
        to take that kind of treatment.
```

The speech tends to dominate visual action and incorporates too many different thoughts, without essential breaks for transitions or reactions. It would be helpful to intersperse reactions and stage directions at the end of each major unit of thought. That makes the speech seem less formidable, and its impact more immediate. Here's what it might look like:

```
                    RITA
                  (to Anne)
        They fired you because you're
        a woman, not for any other reason.
        If you were a man you would have
        been promoted.
```

Anne tries not to pay attention. She's in no mood for Rita's harangue.

```
                    RITA (cont'g)
          Don't let them do that to you.
          Go back and fight for what you
          believe in.

Anne says nothing. Rita sees she's getting nowhere,
crosses over to her friend and speaks softly but urgently.

                    RITA(cont'g)
          I was always warned to look out
          for bigots like that. You've got
          to stand up and let them know you're
          not going to take that kind of treat-
          ment.

A BEAT, then Anne turns to look at her friend. The convic-
tion is sinking in.
```

The idea is to integrate reactions and dialogue in a long pattern of speech, and to trim the "excesses" wherever possible. Long speeches are not always a problem. It might be possible, for example, that Rita blurts out her dialogue in anger and frustration. That reaction might be dramatically imperative and germane to the character's state-of-being. If so, the speech can stand on its own merits.

5. *Too Similar*

Sometimes characters sound the same; their dialogue patterns are indistinguishable from each other. Once that happens the character individuality has been lost. Can you distinguish between these two characters:

```
                    MARILYN
          Hey, did you see the race?

                    EDDIE
          Yeah, I saw the race. They
          were fast, weren't they?

                    MARILYN
          Yeah, they were fast. Did
          ya win?

                    EDDIE
          Nah, not when I needed it.
```

The characters sound precisely the same, and they're redundant on top of it. One way to counter the problem is to provide some psychological richness to the scene. The characters need to be re-examined in terms of motivations, intentions, and sense of urgency. Psychological dimensions might provide a greater dimensional canvas for the creation of dialogue. Since Marilyn and Eddie are two different human beings, their inner thoughts and attitudes might be expressed in totally different dialogue structure. Here's how the scene might play:

```
                    MARILYN
                  (tentatively)
            You saw the race?

Eddie shrugs off the question.

                    EDDIE
            Sure.  They were fast,  Ran
            neck and neck --

                    MARILYN
                  (interrupting)
            Never mind that.  Did you
            win?  Eddie?

No response.  Then:

                    EDDIE
            Not this time.  Not when I
            needed it.
```

When creating dialogue remember that your characters are unique human beings, with ability to interact at the highest levels of subtlety and complexity. One producer told me he covers the names of characters during the first pass at a script, to see if they're drawn dimensionally. If he can't distinguish between the blocks of dialogue, he discards the script as "characterless."

6. Too Stilted

This is dialogue that sounds as if it came from a history book, a poem, a newspaper, a grammar text, but not from a person. This is an example of stilted dialogue:

```
                    ALLEN
            It is my responsibility to
            provide you with my interpre-
            tation of the event.  You are
            the only person that might
            accept that perspective.  You
            must hear me out.
```

Unless Allen has a particularly pedantic problem it would be more effective for him to colloquialize and get to the bottom line quickly:

```
          ALLEN
     You gotta listen to me!
```

And that says it all. Don't be afraid to use contractions in dialogue; that's the way real people speak. It helps to read dialogue aloud, if necessary, to hear the character in action. If the speech pattern is stilted, you can improvise the scene. That might provide a more spontaneous feel to the character's actions and reactions. If you improvise, try putting the same characters into different conflicts. You'll be surprised how much you learn about them.

7. *Too Preachy*

This is a problem related to being "head on," "redundant," "too long," and "too stilted." The character tends to sound very formal, and espouses thematic ideas or philosophical notions. He or she becomes an ideological mouthpiece for the writer rather than a dimensional being. This speech, for example, borders on the preachy side:

```
          MARK
     Do you see what happens when
     criminals run free?  They belong
     in jail or they threaten the
     very fibre of society.  This sort
     of thing would never happen if
     we had stronger lawmakers and
     laws.
```

If a character must speak with strong convictions, it doesn't have to sound like an editorial. Mark can get the same point across by growling:

```
          MARK
     The creep belongs in a cage for
     everyone's protection.  I don't
     care what the law says.
```

The exact nature of the dialogue is, of course, dependent on the unfolding action in the scene, and the consistency of motivations and behavior of the character throughout the story and script.

8. Too Introspective

This problem deals specifically with the character who is alone, and speaks out loud. This cliché is typical:

```
                JUDY
             (to herself)
     Oh, how I long to be with
     him now.
```

That's enough to make any writer cringe. How often does a person actually talk to himself or herself? Not very. And when we do, it's not in complete, logical sentences. Logic is antithetical to the emotion of the moment. The dramatic conventions of a Shakespearean soliloquy are very different from the cinematic expectations of television realism. It makes more sense for the character to take advantage of the private moment on screen through visual convention. She might glance at her fiance's picture, close her eyes, and try to gain back her composure. Once again, actions speak louder than words.

9. Too Inconsistent

This means a character is saying something that doesn't "fit" the personality already created. The dialogue is incongruous with character. In some cases, that inconsistency is due to lack of proper transitions in the scene. This is an example of erratic dialogue or attitudes that change too quickly to be believed.

```
             . DEBBIE
     I wish you would both listen
     to me.

             HOWIE
     No!  David and I have better
     things to do.

             DEBBIE
     I'm telling you this for your
     own good --

             HOWIE
     O.k., we'll do it.
```

The thought transitions are simply too quick to be credible. It might work better if the proper actions and reactions are built into the scene through suggested transitions. This is one way of handling that problem:

> DEBBIE
> I wish you would both listen
> to me.

> HOWIE
> No!

He glances up at his sister, and sees the hurt in her eyes. Then, softer, he tries to explain.

> HOWIE (cont'g)
> David and I have important things
> to do. . .

That obviously has no impact. She tries to control the urgency in her voice.

> DEBBIE
> I'm telling you this for your
> own good --

A long BEAT, then Howie turns away, heading toward the couch. He mulls it over. Finally:

> HOWIE
> O.k., we'll do it.

Debbie breathes a sigh of relief.

Sometimes the problem of inconsistent dialogue can be helped by analyzing the character's inner drives and attitudes on a moment-to-moment basis in the scene. The solution might simply lie in the need for more transitional time; or there might be a need for more thorough character development in the script.

10. Too Unbelievable

This is a catch-all category that implies a character doesn't sound real—for any number of reasons. A writer can test the credibility of dialogue by speaking it aloud, seeing if it rings true. It should sound like a real person responding to the immediate circumstances we've just seen. If there is a problem, try this exercise: put the same characters into a different conflict situation. That kind of written exercise provides a direct conflict of wills, with totally opposing intentions. The two characters might thrash out the conflict in two or three pages. One may give in, one may walk out, both may compromise; the outcome is strictly up to you. However, the dialogue and reactions must integrate, the motivations and behavior must be logical and consistent. Once you know how the individual characters interact, the integrity of the character is assured. The original dialogue can be tested against your heightened insight into motivations, intentions, and attitudes.

PART THREE

THE SCRIPT

7

The Film Script Format

Film Script Format

Most dramatic series and long-form TV projects (mini-series, movies-of-the-week, 120 minute pilots) are shot on film. Since TV films are produced like motion pictures, the script looks exactly the same as a motion picture screenplay: each scene is broken down and described in visual detail; the stage directions and dialogue are single-spaced; the visualization is described in paragraph form.

The more scripts you read, the more familiar you'll become with various styles, forms, and techniques. Professional TV and film scripts are available from special holdings such as the Charles K. Feldman Library at the A.F.I. Center for Advanced Film Studies in Beverly Hills, California (they have thousands of scripts on file), or the Academy of TV Arts & Sciences Library at UCLA. Scripts might also be available from independent production companies.

On the following pages, you'll find a film script model which analyzes the structure and format of a television script. I urge you to examine the sample carefully since it deals with those problems and questions you'll inevitably face.

SAMPLE FILM SCRIPT FORMAT

The title goes here, capitalized and underlined

The Type of Project is in Small Letters, e.g.,
A Series Presentation -- or -- a 120 Feature for TV

A brief description of the nature of the project

by

The Writer's Name

Writer is named here

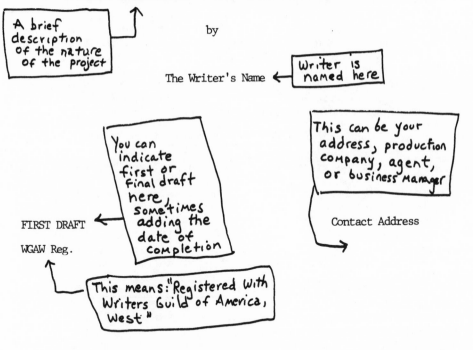

You can indicate first or final draft here, sometimes adding the date of completion

This can be your address, production company, agent, or business manager

FIRST DRAFT

WGAW Reg.

Contact Address

This means: "Registered with Writers Guild of America, West"

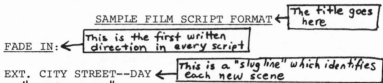

SAMPLE FILM SCRIPT FORMAT ← [The title goes here]

FADE IN: ← [This is the first written direction in every script]

EXT. CITY STREET--DAY ← [This is a "slug line" which identifies each new scene]
  ‖ double-space ‖

This is the way you start a film script, with a succinct
designation in the "slug" line of Exterior or Interior
(use "EXT." or "INT."), the location of the scene
(HOSPITAL PARKING LOT; MACDONALD'S RESTAURANT; DAVID'S
BEDROOM; THE HOTEL BAR; etc.), and the time of day,
i.e., DAY or NIGHT. That information is necessary
for the production unit manager to determine the set
requirements, location requirements, and lighting
requirements of your show.   ‖ double-space implies new angle ‖

[locations, actions, and characters are described here]

Sometimes you can simply skip a paragraph to describe
another angle in the scene, without actually having to
label it above. This is particularly true if you are
thinking of a related piece of stage action in a master shot, or wide shot. This saves you from "over-
directing" your script, and permits ease of reading.

ANGLE ON PARKED CAR ← [you can specify an angle this way]

You should use specific angles when you want to focus
our attention on a specific visual item--objects, people,
P.O.V.'s (Points of View). This helps move your plot
forward in a linear fashion. Note that the above angle
does not have to include any other slug-line references
(e.g., DAY/NIGHT), because it is still part of the same
scene (EXT. CITY STREET--DAY). You are merely calling
for a different angle within that scene.

INT. CAR--DAY ← [this indicates a different scene and location]

If you change the physical locale of the scene, you
must provide a new slug line. You'll note that it isn't
necessary to put "CUT TO" from the previous scene,
because it is still part of a related visual sequence,
occurring at the same time and place.

When you describe your CHARACTERS or any information
pertaining to CAMERA SHOTS, be sure to cap that information. Try to be as visual as you can in your description

of the CHARACTERS--who they are, what they look like, what they're doing at the moment we see them. Don't forget the setting in the scene. You'll have to describe it in vivid detail, to give a rich and clear picture of the mood, atmosphere, and dramatic action.

> *This is how to set up dialogue*

                    JANET
      Let's move on to something else, O.K.?
      How about the shot numbering system?

                    TOM
                 (mock disgust)

> *parenthetical directions can be used to clarify an attitude or interpretation*

      You mean numbering all of the camera shots?
      Forget it! That's done by the production
      secretary after the final shooting script is
      turned in. Writers don't have to be concerned
      with that. Directors will want to change it,
      anyway.

> *This is one way to indicate reactions*

JANET shrugs, starts the car, and pulls away.

EXT. STREET--DAY

> *a new location and scene*

We see the car pulling away from the curb, and disappearing down the street in light traffic. Notice that
it is necessary to provide a new slug-line, because we
are now shooting outside again. If we CUT back to
JANET and TOM in their car, we would have to designate
another INT. CAR--DAY description. But we can use
another technique to keep the dialogue alive, and the
visuals wide open. That's the use of "V.O." (VOICE
OVER) or "O.S." (OFF SCREEN).

                    JANET (V.O.)

> *here's how to indicate "voice over"*

      So, while you see the car pulling down the
      street, you can still hear me talking.

                    TOM (V.O.)
      Incidentally, there is a technical difference
      between the voice over and the off-screen voice.
      The V.O. is generally used like this or some-
      times by a Narrator. The O.S. is used when one
      of the characters isn't seen in the shot but
      we know he or she is in the scene, perhaps on
      the other side of the room.

                   JANET (V.O.)
       That's confusing. No wonder a lot of writers
       are just using V.O.'s all the time.

HIGH ANGLE ← *a new angle in the same scene (EXT. STREET-DAY)*

here's the scene description

From an AERIAL SHOT, we see the car blend into the
light maze of traffic on the city streets. ← *this indicates the end of one sequence of action, and the need for a new scene and location*

                 CUT TO

EXT. BEACH--NIGHT ← *here's the new scene*

We're in a totally different location now, so the first
thing you must do is describe it. Try to set the right
visual and emotional atmosphere with your description.
If we see TOM and JANET, do they look tired after driv-
ing all day? Are they wearing different clothes? Are
they tense? bored? anxious? happy?

CLOSE UP--TOM ← *one way of indicating a CLOSE UP*

The CLOSE UP can be called in a number of ways, <u>e.g.,</u> *reactions are described here*
CU TOM, CLOSE ON TOM, or simply: TOM. Now you describe
what the CU reveals. Perhaps it is a look of concern.

TOM'S P.O.V.--DOWN THE BEACH ← *one way of indicating "point of view"*

here's what the character sees

In the distance, he sees the light of a bonfire. Several
FIGURES are huddled nearby. Note that the point-of-view
shot clearly describes what the character sees.

                 JANET (O.S. ← *this is how to indicate "off screen" dialogue*
       Tom? What's the matter?

BACK TO SHOT ← *one way of returning to a previous shot*

This designation simply calls for scene's prior establishing shot. You might also use ANGLE ON TOM AND JANET,
which calls for a shot featuring both characters.

                 TOM   *parenthetical directions under a character's name should be short*
                (tense) ←
       Nothing's the matter.

The parenthetical information should be used if the
attitude of the character is not clear by dialogue
alone.　It wouldn't be necessary for you to say TOM
speaks angrily if he shouts "Get out of here!"　You
might also include some relevant stage business for
the character, if this can be done succinctly.　For
the most part, however, try to let the dialogue speak
for itself.　Stage directions can generally be incorporated in this space.　For example:　JANET glances
down the beach, squints to see the bonfire O.S.
(off screen), and looks back at TOM.　A BEAT, then
she packs their belongings hurriedly.

> A "BEAT" is described here

                    JANET
        Let's go.

The "Beat" that was used above is a filmic version
of the dramatic pause, or the Chekovian pause.　It
implies a second or two for the character to digest
the information, before he or she acts on it.

NEW ANGLE　← another way of calling a shot in the scene

This is a legitimate angle designation, which implies
a different camera angle from the previous one.　You
don't have to specify the shot, but you should describe
the action taking place.　Note, too, that if some
background action is occurring, you identify it as
"b.g." (not spelled out); similarly, if camera is
focused on foreground action, you would say f.g.　← "foreground"

ANGLE ON THE CAR

JANET and TOM **trot** through the beach to their car, and
hastily climb in.　She starts it up, but the engine won't
start.　In the b.g., we can make out the FIGURES by the
bonfire, moving toward them. ← "background"

                    FRED
        Hurry!

A BEAT before the ignition catches, then the car starts
up and skids away.　Note that the character doesn't
have to repeat any visual information, i.e., he wouldn't

say "Hurry, the figures are coming toward us!" We
can assume that JANET sees the same thing he does.

When you have special sound effects, <u>e.g.</u>, the waves
crashing, the fire crackling, etc., you can place
those directly in the scene description to add atmosphere and mood to the piece. Keep the action moving
from scene to scene, and be sure your characters act
and react like real people. Each one is unique, and
must sound and behave like a credible, identifiable
person. Once the script is finished, be sure to:

all effects--visual and
sound -- are incorporated
into the scene description

FADE OUT.

This is the last
direction in the
script. The
screen image
fades to black.

• • •

Typewriter Settings for a Film Script

Margins for a film script are generally set according to these guidelines. Most scripts are typed in standard (*Pica*) type on 8½″ × 11″ manuscript paper.

	Pica Type	Elite Type
New Scenes and Stage Directions		
Left Margin	20	24
Right Margin	75	90
Dialogue	30	36
Name Above Dialogue	40	48

Capitalizing in the Script

Words are generally capitalized to identify NEW SCENES, NEW CAMERA ANGLES or SHOTS, and any SPECIAL EFFECTS (camera or sound effects). The names of CHARACTERS are also capitalized to indicate who is performing in the scene, and who is speaking at the moment (if a character's name is part of the speech it is *not* capitalized).

There is some latitude about capitalizing a character's name throughout the script. Some writers will only capitalize it the first time the character appears in the script. Others will capitalize the name throughout each scene in the script. Both ways are considered acceptable.

The reasons for capitalizing are pragmatic. It helps the director and production manager break down the script for new scenes and location requirements, camera and lighting needs, rehearsal schedules, shooting schedules, and so on.

How to Structure a Scene

A scene is one link in a dramatic sequence of events. It is comprised of action and dialogue that occurs in a single place and time. Once the location changes, so does the scene. The dictates of the story determine how long each scene will be, but many writers try to economize. Some scenes may run a few sentences, others as long as a few pages.

Here is a dramatic sequence which takes place at the airport. It is actually comprised of three separate scenes:

1. outside the airport
2. inside the terminal
3. inside the baggage compartment

Within each scene, a number of different camera angles and shots may be required to put the sequence together. But the general location remains the same, and the production crew will not have to move elsewhere.

①   EXT. AIRPORT--DAY

We're at L. A. Airport, clogged with traffic,
the lines of cars backed up as far as we can
see. A large 707 sits waiting for take-off
at one of the terminals.

②   INT. TERMINAL--DAY

As busy inside as it was outside. Lots of
people milling around waiting for the word to
board the plane to Washington. A small coterie
of FIRST CLASS PASSENGERS make their way into
the plane, obviously important. They're government V.I.P.'s.

In another section of the terminal, watching
the action, are THREE MEN near a food stand.
One wears a suit and tie, the others wear
baggage handling outfits. The MAN IN THE SUIT
slips open his attache and manages to pass
some wiring to the BAGGAGE HANDLER. A quick
glance around. No one has seen them. We HEAR
the call over the P.A. system for all passengers to board the flight. The MAN IN THE SUIT,
attache firmly in hand, waits on line for the
security check. He passes through the gates
without a problem.

③   INT. PLANE'S BAGGAGE COMPARTMENT--DAY

The two BAGGAGE HANDLERS work furiously to
attach wires to the wall of the compartment.
One HANDLER opens a plaid piece of luggage,
exposing some kind of electronic device.
Time is pressing, but they complete their
mission. One of them reaches down into the
luggage and snaps a switch. The countdown
has begun. They scramble out of the compartment and slam the door shut, leaving us in
darkness.

The *first* scene—outside the airport—is an *establishing shot* which
provides a visual orientation to the viewer. When the scene is shot, the
director may use a number of different angles (a HIGH ANGLE of the

Airport, VARIOUS ANGLES of the traffic, a CLOSE UP of the large 707, etc.) But the actual scene location does not change (EXT. AIR-PORT—DAY).

The *second* scene takes place inside the terminal. The director may use a number of different *set-ups* (camera angles and lighting changes) to achieve the total effect of passengers waiting, men interacting, passengers boarding, and so on.

The *third* scene takes place in the baggage compartment, and completes the dramatic action in the chain of events. The scene's action is specifically related to the previous scenes in the sequence.

Scenes are plotted carefully to provide the full impact of an unfolding story. They are both visual and dramatic structures to help build the effectiveness of the larger acts.

How to Structure an Act

The development of an Act rests on the established principles of story-plotting and scene construction—hook the audience early, and build the action and conflict at a steady pace. The entire story has to be told within the parameters of a given number of acts and a limited number of script pages.

The audience interest curve is especially helpful in conceptualizing the story needs for each act. A writer can block out the major crisis point in each act and build the story conflict accordingly:

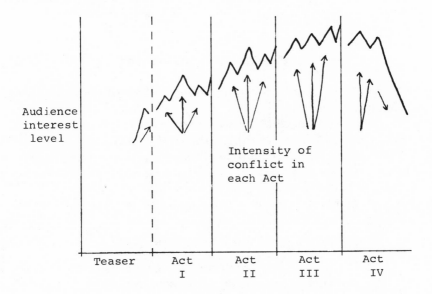

With the interest curve in mind, the writer can examine the function of each act and determine its effectiveness in the total plot structure. You can see whether an act sustains or builds audience interest, and whether it makes effective use of dramatic action points throughout the show. Many shows begin with a short "teaser" which hooks audience interest in 3–4 minutes. Then the script builds the story with 12–14 minutes of plotting for each act, at an increased intensity throughout the script. The end of an act usually peaks audience interest (to hold viewers throughout the commercial) and reflects a natural break in the story line.

Here's a very broad picture of the act structure, based loosely on Jerome Coopersmith's informative "script table" in *Professional Writer's Teleplay/Screenplay Format* (available from writers Guild of America, East). Keep in mind that these are just rough guidelines to provide a sense of the act structure and length in a television show.

LENGTH OF SCRIPT:	*TEASER:*	*ACTS:*
30-minute show	(*optional*)	I, II
(about 30 pp.)	(3–6 pp.)	(about 13–15 pp. each)
60-minute show	(*optional*)	I, II, III, IV
(about 60 pp.)	(4–8 pp.)	(about 14–15 pp. each)
90-minute show	(*optional*)	I, II, III, IV, V, VI
(about 90–110 pp.)	(4–8 pp.)	(about 14–18 pp. each)

In the case of a 120-minute film, the script is generally written without any Teasers or Act structure. It's structured like a feature film with an open-ended story approach and can run from 120–140 pages.

How to Write Camera Angles

Most television scripts are written *without* complicated, extensive camera directions.

There is no need to clutter scripts with OVER-THE-SHOULDER SHOTS, REVERSE ANGLES, MEDIUM SHOTS, or TWO SHOTS. The director will make all those decisions in pre-production planning. It's the writer's responsibility to merely suggest the *potential* for camera coverage without complicating or over-directing the script.

Here are a few angles which are particularly helpful in scripting:

WIDE ANGLE: This provides full screen coverage of all the ensuing action. It's also called a FULL SHOT.

NEW ANGLE: This suggests that some other perspective is needed, but does not necessarily pinpoint that coverage.

CLOSE UP: This is the magnified coverage of a person's face or a specific object on screen.

BACK TO SHOT: This is a way of suggesting that a previous angle is called for.

ANGLE ON . . . . : This might focus attention on a specific place or person (*e.g.* ANGLE ON HALLWAY or ANGLE ON HARRIET).

The following is from a television film called "Death's Head." You can see how simply the angles are set up for the opening sequence in the script.

```
FADE IN:

INT. CAROL'S BEDROOM--NIGHT

It's late at night, and we can barely make out the
figure of a woman sleeping alone in a king-size bed.
She's cuddled up under the covers, the other half
of the bed remains untouched.  A shaft of light
seeps in from the hall  highlighting her face as
she stirs...CAROL MADDEN is a striking woman...early
30's, long blonde hair, soft compelling features.

Over the STEADY RHYTHM of the air conditioner, we
hear a SLIGHT RUSTLE.  It doesn't seem to disturb
her...But then, after a Beat, we hear another
RUSTLING SOUND.  Tired, CAROL opens her eyes...
inquisitive at first, not really sure if she's
heard anything.

CLOSE ANGLE ON BED

A huge black spider is crawling across the covers,
gliding slowly and methodically toward her.

CLOSE-UP CAROL

She sees it, recoils in fear.

                                        CUT TO:

INT. DOWNSTAIR'S DEN--NIGHT

CLOSE ANGLE ON CRATE

The black furry legs of a spider can be seen trying
to climb the ledge of the crate.  A hand gently
cups the insect, and adroitly puts it back into
the crate, closing the cover.
```

```
NEW ANGLE

We see CAROL's husband, STEVE, in the brightly lit
room downstairs.  The wood-panelled Den sports a
good many insect displays on walls and table...
exotic butterflies, beetles, moths, all artfully
pinned and exhibited under glass.  There's a
peculiar beauty about the whole collection.  STEVE,
a slightly built, but good-looking man in his late
40's, is straightening up from the small wooden
crate beside him.  He glances around, looking for
something.  One of the spiders is missing.
```

•   •   •

If you analyze the script structure and camera angles, here's what you'll find:

1. The "slug-line" identifies individual scenes (INT. CAROL'S BEDROOM—NIGHT; INT. DEN—NIGHT).
2. Each scene is comprised of different shots or camera angles. So when we describe Carol's bedroom, then cut to a close-up of the spider on the bed, we are still in the same scene. We simply changed the viewing perspective.
3. Camera angles are suggested clearly. The description of CAROL'S BEDROOM is an implied WIDE ANGLE which establishes all the action in the scene. CLOSE ANGLES are used for special dramatic emphasis and impact. NEW ANGLES imply different perspectives within the same scene. Sometimes NEW ANGLES are implied by simply skipping a paragraph in the scene description.
4. The scene descriptions provide exact visual information about the set, character, and stage action. The descriptions tell us exactly what the camera sees.
5. The camera coverage and special effects are capitalized; so are the characters' names. Capitalizing is not mandatory, but it does help in pre-production breakdown of the script.

How to Write Special Sequences:
Intercuts, Montages, Dreams, and Flashbacks

1. Intercuts

Intercutting is switching back and forth between two or more scenes consecutively. For example, a script may call for parallel action and dialogue during a phone conversation. If the writer plays the scene in one location, it could result in static dramatic action. If the script cuts back and forth between characters, it might result in awkward repetitions of scene descriptions.

The most common solution to this kind of problem is to identify the on-going scenes in advance by calling for an INTERCUT SEQUENCE. The appropriate scenes are defined while action and dialogue are written as usual. The last scene concludes with: END INTERCUT SEQUENCE. This is what it looks like:

NOTE: INTERCUT SEQUENCE:

INT. LAURA'S APT.--DAY

She's on the phone in the den, pictures scattered all over the floor.

EXT. PHONE BOOTH--DAY

It's raining cats and dogs as we see MIKE, drenched to the bone, talking to LAURA.

>   LAURA
>   (into phone)
>   Hello?

>   MIKE
>   (into phone)
>   Hi, Laura, It's me. You o.k.?

>   LAURA
>   (into phone)
>   Fine, but I miss you somethin' awful.
>   When will you come back?

He takes a deep breath. Then, trying to sound casual:

>   MIKE
>   (into phone)
>   Not for a long time.

LAURA's eyes widen. She didn't want to hear that.

END INTERCUT SEQUENCE.

The need for an intercut sequence is dictated by the length of the required scene and the importance of seeing consecutive dramatic action on the screen. The sequence allows the director to edit as he or she sees fit.

2. Montages

A *montage* is a succession of different shots that seem to condense time, emotions, and action in just a few short scenes. The story may call for a quickly established romance, or an historical progression of images leading to the present time.

As with intercuts, the montage is identified in advance of the sequence and at its conclusion. The individual scenes are sometimes listed by number (although this is not always the case).

If a writer needs to show a character undertaking different activities in a progression of time, the montage sequence is ideal. This is one way it would be set up:

<u>MONTAGE SEQUENCE</u>:

1. INT. CAROL'S ROOM--DAY

She's cleaning it up, carefully straightening the sheets on the bed.

2. EXT. SUPERMARKET--DAY

She wheels a basket down the aisles, quickly pulling food from the counter, and piling it into the basket.

3. INT. CAROL'S KITCHEN--DAY

A bandana over her head, she's polishing the oven fast and furiously.

4. EXT. CAROL'S PORCH--NIGHT

She's in her jeans collapsed on the swinging porch bench, tired and weary.

<u>END MONTAGE</u>

There's no need to show Carol cleaning up everything in the room, or conversing with the cashier at the supermarket. The visual information in a montage implicitly gives the viewer that sense of completed action.

3. Dreams and Fantasies

In scriptwriting, *dreams* and *fantasies* are used interchangeably. They permit the viewer to enter the character's mind, to literally see imagination, daydreams, fantasies, nightmares.

If a dream sequence is short and fleeting, it can be distinguished from "real time" by inserting specific parenthetical information. For example:

```
CU CAROL

She's fast asleep, a look of anxiety twists her face.
Clearly disturbed, restless...

CU SPIDER (DREAM SEQUENCE)

It crawls toward her at an inscrutably slow pace...

CU CAROL (BACK TO REALITY)

She snaps her eyes open and looks around.   There's
nothing there.
```

In this case, the dream sequence shot is almost a *flashcut, i.e.* it is a very fast insert into the "real" world—Carol sleeping.

If a dream or fantasy is longer, the entire sequence might be distinguished from "real time." That practice minimizes the chance of confusing the reader. A longer sequence is generally identified in advance, and the first "real" scene is also identified.

Here's what a longer dream sequence—or fantasy sequence—looks like:

```
CU CAROL
She's fast asleep, a look of anxiety twists her face.
Clearly disturbed, restless...

                                        DISSOLVE TO:


DREAM SEQUENCE

EXT. MARINA VILLAGE--TWILIGHT

We hear an eerie, toneless quality to the b.g. music
from the village shops...This is a distorted, night-
marish replay of her first visit...

ANGLE ON GIRL
```

A young GIRL beckons to her from one of the shops. The
GIRL is hawking something, we're not sure what. CAROL
moves curiously toward her, in SLOW MOTION...

INT. SHOP--TWILIGHT

CAROL enters the shop, looks around, sees the young
GIRL behind the counter, back to camera. She turns to
face CAROL...

CLOSE UP--CAROL

Her face reflects shock, her eyes widen in horror as
she sees...

HER P.O.V.--EXTREME CLOSEUP--GIRL

The GIRL has become a TOOTHLESS OLD HAG. We're on a
DISTORTED FISH EYE LENS...the HAG beckons to CAROL,
smiling bizarrely...We see the sign of a hexagon
dangling from her neck, shimmering...The OLD HAG
continues to beckon, drawing her closer...

EXTREME CLOSEUP--CAROL

She shrieks in fear.

<u>END DREAM SEQUENCE</u>

                                                   CUT TO:

INT. CAROL'S BEDROOM--NIGHT (REALITY)

She is sitting up in bed, screaming, frightened...stops.
Looks around the room...silence...

The entire dream sequence is played out in two scenes: EXT.
MARINA VILLAGE and INT. SHOP. The various angles and visual
descriptions help set the mood and atmosphere. Once the sequence is
over, the "real time" sequence picks up the pace and helps sustain the
mood.

4. Flashbacks

A flashback distinguishes "time remembered" from real time and is
set up like the dream sequence. If a memory is very brief, the writer
can parenthetically identify the FLASHBACK. For example:

CU RONALD

He remembers something, the memory plagues him.

INT. ATTIC--NIGHT (FLASHBACK)

It's a dingy place, no air, no light. In the corner,
something moves...We can't make it out, but it's alive.

ANGLE ON RONALD (FLASHBACK)

He's on his knees, a flashlight in hand. He tries to
switch it on, but the batteries are dead. He throws
it toward the moving object, and races toward the
attic steps.

CU RONALD (REALITY)

Jarred by the memory.

If the FLASHBACK SEQUENCE is much longer, it would be written just like the longer Dream Sequence.

This might be the time to caution against the unnecessary use of flashbacks. The technique is helpful to provide some exposition about characters or to establish a "backstory" to the plot. However, if it's used too often, the effect can be detrimental to the story. The more a writer relies on Flashbacks, the more he or she intrudes on the forward thrust of the plot. If a story begins in the present tense, then slips back in time, the viewer already knows the outcome. The audience is waiting to see the characters work their way out of the current situation; that action is forestalled with the intrusion of flashbacks. A television script must gain the viewer's interest quickly, and—unlike a Fellini film—hold audience interest throughout commercial breaks. If you must use flashbacks, do so sparingly. They may lead you to believe the story is progressing nicely, when in fact it's stopped the plot cold.

8

Visual Descriptions and the Master Scene Script

Writing Effective Scene Descriptions

In a television script, entire sequences are created and defined according to cinematic perspectives and dramatic needs. Every scene of every act is richly described. Locales are defined from the camera's perspective; stage actions and reactions are visually presented; characters are dimensionally drawn. The script's imagery and atmosphere are derived directly from the scene descriptions and stage directions.

Some writers are concerned about including too much (or too little) information in scene descriptions. Each scene requires its own analysis in the context of the larger act. Visual descriptions should be long enough to establish the full flavor of the place and action; short enough to keep the pacing alive and the reader interested in the story flow.

Just as there are problems in dialogue, so there are predictable pitfalls in scene descriptions. These are some of the more common stylistic problems.

Some scene descriptions are written too *choppily,* presumably to account for each piece of stage business. Here's an example of that problem:

```
Marsha picks up the garbage.  She stops to feed
the dog.  She goes to the back door.
```

The writing style can be smoothed out by avoiding separate sentence units and excessive use of pronouns. The action can be described more comprehensively:

```
Marsha picks up the garbage, stops to feed the
dog, then continues on her way out the back door.
```

A similar problem occurs when a number of different characters are in a scene, and the writer wants to keep them alive. The tendency for *pronoun confusion* increases with the number of characters interacting in the sequence. For example:

```
The dog barks.  Steve enters.  Marsha sees him
and tries to calm him.  She gets him a drink from
the bar and he barks louder.
```

Confusing to say the least. The problems can be corrected by addressing the specific characters and compressing the action:

```
As Steve enters, Marsha tries to calm the barking
dog.  Unsuccessful, she heads toward the bar and
gets Steve a drink.  The dog barks louder.
```

A related problem is *redundancy* in visual description. A number of key words might be repeated needlessly. It helps to "flag" those words, *i.e.* literally circle them to see if they intrude on the reading flow:

```
Marsha smiles and he smiles back.  Steve crosses
to the fireplace and he starts the fire and lights
the wood.  He pokes the fire with brass tongs and
the fire begins to crackle.
```

The stage directions need to be smoothed out. The phrasing can be modified and polished:

```
They exchange smiles as Steve crosses to the
fireplace.  He lights the wood, pokes the brass
tongs into the flames.  The fire begins to crackle.
```

Limiting the amount of repetition—in both words and phrases—cleans up the description and makes the script more readable.

There is often a question raised about naming real places in the scene, as opposed to creating a fictional environment. If the environment needs a special quality, by all means it should be created. However, there is nothing wrong with incorporating a recognizable entity in the scene. If a character waits under the arch of MacDonald's restaurant, or is trying to find parking near the White House, real images are conjured up. The locations have a built-in value for immediate identification.

A different problem arises if a writer wants to incorporate current events, recognizable names, or contemporary songs in the script. Aside from the issue of rights and clearances, that event, person, or song might fade into oblivion by the time the script is ready to be produced. As for music, unless a particular song is *critical* to the needs of a script, it is wise to avoid the frustration and legal hassles involved. A writer can simply suggest a song style rather than provide someone else's lyrics. For example:

```
In the b.g. (background] we hear the strains of a
blues song, and the husky voice of a nightclub
vocalist.  Over the song, we hear the din of the
supper club crowd, ignoring the music behind them.
```

This scene description sets atmosphere, without defining the song or the lyrics. On the other hand, some writers deliberately choose a dated reference to establish the period atmosphere of a piece. The appropriateness is determined by the needs of a specific project, and the artistic style of the individual writer.

A writer's style is partially determined by the images used in scene descriptions. Two writers can approach the same idea with dramatically different results. One may have the viewer on the edge of his seat in suspense; another may have him rolling in the aisles with laughter. Both may be telling the same story. A writer who is adept at visual description greatly enhances the mood and atmospheric values of a script.

Writing the Master Scene Script

Most original television scripts are submitted in the Master Scene form as opposed to shooting script form. A Master Scene script is one that offers a vivid description of action within each scene, but does not break down specific camera angles or shots; nor does it number the shots in the margins.

In the Master Scene script, the visual descriptions are particularly important. The script allows latitude for the integration of character and action, without the encumbrance of complex camera coverage.

The following script serves as a good example of the readability and visual effectiveness of a Master Scene script. The excerpt is from a television film called "Disappearing Act." In the script, CAPT. DAN is an old retired cop, AL SILVERMAN is a young clerk from Missing Persons Bureau, and JOYCE KESSLER is his partner. They are determined to find out what happened to a missing subway train full of people. In the process, they are stalked by adversaries as well as police.

The excerpt opens in a SUBWAY TUNNEL at night where the three featured characters are searching for the missing subway. We are picking up the action in the middle of a scene as indicated by the CONTINUED on top of the page. Note the relative scarcity of camera shots and the strong visualization in the scene descriptions.

CONTINUED:

They begin crossing through the maze of tracks.

                    CAPT. DAN
          Careful now. Watch the wooden rail,
          that's the live one.

                    SILVERMAN
          Are you sure this is right? Let's see
          the map.

                    JOYCE
          If we get run over by an A-Train, we
          went wrong.

Capt. Dan takes the map out of his pocket and Silverman
holds the flashlight. It is a normal Transit Riders
Map and shows almost no significant detail. As they
stand in the maze of tracks a rumble is heard growing
rapidly louder.

                    JOYCE
                 (frightened)
          Which way is it coming from?

                    SILVERMAN
                 (panicking)
          I don't know.

                    CAPT. DAN
          Get the lead out!

Capt. Dan hop-scotches across the rails towards a small depression in the tunnel wall. Silverman follows, dragging Joyce by the hand. Before he has made it a headlight flashes around the bend and a train roars straight toward them. Joyce screams and grabs Silverman as they both flatten themselves against the wall, trying to squeeze into the too small alcove. The train roars straight for them and at the last instant veers left, passing within twelve inches of their bodies as it negotiates a sharp curve.

> JOYCE
> (panting uncontrollably)
> Oh my God...

> SILVERMAN
> Shhh, it's all right, calm down.

He strokes her to calm her down.

> CAPT. DAN
> At least we know they can't sneak up
> on us. We'll always have enough warnin'.

INT. DARK TUNNEL--NIGHT

Illuminated only by an occasional low wattage lightbulb, this tunnel is smaller, darker, danker than the one before. We can barely make out our three heroes as they approach. Capt. Dan's limp is becoming more pronounced. Silverman shines his light ahead.

> SILVERMAN
> I can see another set of switches up
> there, must be where the Far Rockaway line
> cuts off.

> CAPT. DAN
> Let me set a minute, this damp air has
> got me winded.

He leans against a tool box next to the wall. Joyce looks around, notices water dripping from above, mud all over her shoes. Another rumble is heard.

> SILVERMAN
> Behind the tool box!

They run to where Capt. Dan is sitting and hunch down
in the shadow of the large wooden bin. We see the flashlight drop from Silverman's pocket and fall between the
rails.

> JOYCE
>
> Al, the light...

Before he can retrieve it the train comes roaring
through. In the small tunnel wind howls by their ears
and the noise is deafening. They close their eyes as
whirlwinds of grit, soot, and dirt pockmark their faces.

CLOSE UP--JOYCE
She opens her eyes and tries to adjust to the near
blackness, her eyes widening in terror.

P.O.V. JOYCE
Dozens of luminous, close-set pink eyes stare back at
her.

CLOSE UP--JOYCE
She screams at the top of her lungs.

Silverman lunges for the flashlight, turns it on in
time to see a pack of white albino cats glide noise-
lessly across the rails and disappear.

> CAPT. DAN
>
> Just cats, thousands of em live in the
> tunnels and never see the light of day.

INT. CONVERGENCE OF TUNNELS AT SWITCHING POINT--NIGHT

Here the passageway widens as two other lines feed in and
exit from a common point. Silverman, Joyce and Capt. Dan
gingerly begin picking their way across the rails.

> JOYCE
>
> My shoes are so muddy it's like walking
> on suction cups.

> SILVERMAN
>
> I don't ever remember walking on suction
> cups.

> CAPT. DAN
>
> Shhh. Hear that clanking?

They stop and listen. Suddenly it stops. Then it begins
again.

                         SILVERMAN
           What is it?

                         CAPT. DAN
           Shhhh.

Now we hear it again, this time more distinctly. It
sounds like canteens banging against the paraphanalia
that soldiers always wear. Before they can answer the
question they see several flashlight beams approaching
from two different tunnels. Now we see uniformed police-
men running towards them from the distance.

                           COPS
                        (distant)
           There they are.

                           COP
                     (through bullhorn)
           Okay, stay where you are.

Silverman, Joyce, Capt. Dan stand in shock .

                         SILVERMAN
           Come on!

                         CAPT. DAN
                    (gasping for breath)
           I can't make it. You two go ahead and I'll
           turn myself in.

                           JOYCE
           No!

                         CAPT. DAN
           No time for sentiment, get going.

Silverman turns to run but hesitates.

                         CAPT. DAN
           GO!!!

Silverman grabs Joyce and they run. A flare goes off
showing a line of cops closing in from all directions.

COP
(bullhorn)

There's no way out. Put your hands up
and remain where you are.

A rumble reverberates through the tunnel. Capt. Dan
raises his hands and walks toward them.

CAPT. DAN
(gasping)

Hold it boys, I'm coming out.

At this a train roars through from behind Capt. Dan
heading for the cops. It is on the opposite rail but
has the effect of splitting the body of men in two and
adding to the confusion.

A particularly hefty cop in full battle dress runs forward into the light caused by the flare. He wears a huge
cartridge belt hung with every conceivable kind of wea-
pon plus a helmet with face shield. He reaches Capt.
Dan and brutally knocks the old man aside with the
butt of his gas gun, kneels in firing position and
fires a shell at CAMERA. Though we don't see his face
too clearly, his shape is that of Sgt. Santucci.

It explodes behind Silverman and Joyce and they turn to
face him, choking in the fumes.

JOYCE
(coughing)

My shoe! I lost my shoe!

The hefty cop charges forward, his gas rifle dangling
down from one hand, and a raised club over his head.
His fat bounces and his teeth are clenched in eager
anticipation of striking a blow at Silverman and Joyce.

Silverman steps in front of Joyce to protect her. The
hefty cop is about to bring his club crashing into
Silverman's skull when he trips over Joyce's shoe, los-
ing his balance.

He falls forward but quickly regains his balance. In
the process the metal barrel of his gas gun strikes
the third rail, causing a bright blue spark. An instant

later another flare bathes him in brilliant white light.
He stands frozen.

Under the sound of the roaring train comes the faint,
short beginnings of a strangulated scream that is never
finished. Santucci's whole body begins convulsing in
spasms. Smoke rises from his clothes.

Joyce looks on in horror, begins screaming. Silverman
grabs her and drags her, screaming and hysterical, back
into the tunnel.

The train passes and the disorganized force begins to
regroup.

                    COP ONE (O.S.)
          What smells?

                    COP TWO (O.S.)
          Get an ambulance. Get an ambulance!

The smoke clears. Silverman and Joyce have disappeared.

INT. ANOTHER TUNNEL, SMALLER AND DARKER--NIGHT

Joyce leans against the wall, shaking and sobbing.
Silverman stands beside her, pale and weak.

                    SILVERMAN
          We've got to keep going. We're bound to
          come to a station where we can get out.

                    JOYCE
                 (uncontrollably)
          I want to go home, please get me out of here.
          Please, I want to go home. I want to go home.

●   ●   ●

    The visual style of the writer can come through in a Master Scene
script, which relies on *few* camera directions and on a *great deal* of scene
description. Most scripts submitted in the marketplace are in the Master Scene form.

    Once the first draft of a Master Scene script is written, the writer
faces the arduous, intensive task of rewriting. The pacing and atmosphere are analyzed and the story and character development are
probed. However, before we talk about the rewriting process, let's look
at the writing format for live-tape productions.

9

The Videotape Script Format

The Wide Margin Format

If a program is to be produced on videotape, writers use a spacious format that was developed during the early days of live television. The format uses less camera coverage and fewer angles than film scripts. Moreover, everything on the page is double-spaced—stage directions, scene descriptions, and dialogue. The margins are wider, too (15–75 in *Pica* Type; 18–90 in *Elite* Type). That wide-margin and double-space format allows the director plenty of room to jot down technical directions.

Since the script is so spacious, the page count is much longer than film—by *half*. A one hour script in film runs 60 pages; in videotape it might run 90 pages. A two hour film script is about 120 pages; a two hour videotape script is about 180 pages.

The following script model provides a look at the structure and format of a wide margin script, which is appropriate for any videotape drama, comedy, or live action program. Be sure to read through the sample carefully, since it answers questions you might have about setting up a script of your own.

SAMPLE VIDEOTAPE SCRIPT FORMAT ← Title

by

A Writer for TV ← Writer's name

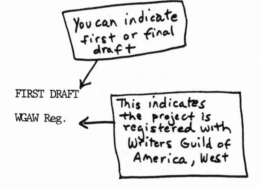

You can indicate first or final draft

FIRST DRAFT

WGAW Reg. ← This indicates the project is registered with Writers Guild of America, West

Contact Address

Your address, production company, agent, or business manager

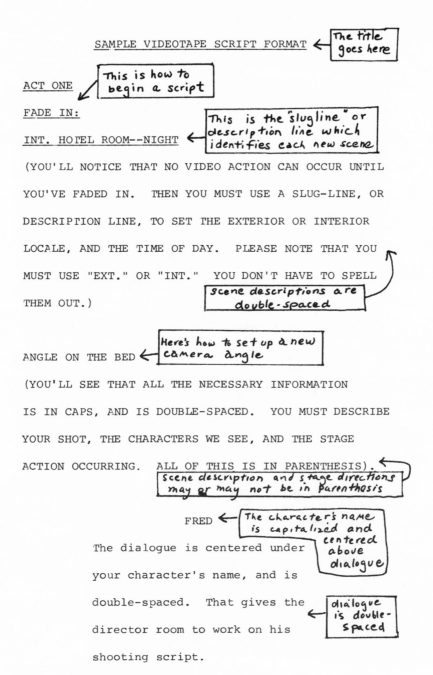

SAMPLE VIDEOTAPE SCRIPT FORMAT ← The title goes here

ACT ONE ← This is how to begin a script

FADE IN:

INT. HOTEL ROOM--NIGHT ← This is the "slugline" or description line which identifies each new scene

(YOU'LL NOTICE THAT NO VIDEO ACTION CAN OCCUR UNTIL YOU'VE FADED IN. THEN YOU MUST USE A SLUG-LINE, OR DESCRIPTION LINE, TO SET THE EXTERIOR OR INTERIOR LOCALE, AND THE TIME OF DAY. PLEASE NOTE THAT YOU MUST USE "EXT." OR "INT." YOU DON'T HAVE TO SPELL THEM OUT.) ← scene descriptions are double-spaced

ANGLE ON THE BED ← Here's how to set up a new camera angle

(YOU'LL SEE THAT ALL THE NECESSARY INFORMATION IS IN CAPS, AND IS DOUBLE-SPACED. YOU MUST DESCRIBE YOUR SHOT, THE CHARACTERS WE SEE, AND THE STAGE ACTION OCCURRING. ALL OF THIS IS IN PARENTHESIS). ← scene description and stage directions may or may not be in parenthesis

FRED ← The character's name is capitalized and centered above dialogue

The dialogue is centered under your character's name, and is double-spaced. That gives the ← dialogue is double-spaced

director room to work on his

shooting script.

-2-

CONTINUED

LINDA

(SMILING)

> Character reactions can be suggested in parenthesis or written in the stage directions

It also allows the actor and producer

to see the lines at a glance.

(BE SURE TO INCLUDE ANY REACTIONS YOUR CHARACTERS

MAY HAVE TO THE PREVIOUS LINES OR ON-GOING ACTION.)

CLOSE UP--FRED

> Here's how to write a "Close-UP." It is also written "C.U.-FRED".

(THIS IS WHERE YOU DESCRIBE HOW YOUR CHARACTER

LOOKS IN A GIVEN SITUATION. HOW DOES HE FEEL

ABOUT THIS MOMENT IN THE SCENE? IT COULD BE A

VERY TELLING REACTION, BUT MUST BE CONSISTENT

WITH THE WAY HE'S ACTED BEFORE.)

> writers often suggest new angles, without "over directing"

WIDE SHOT OF THE BED

(TRY NOT TO "OVER-DIRECT" THE SCENE WITH A LOT OF

CAMERA DIRECTIONS. THIS IS THE RESPONSIBILITY

OF THE DIRECTOR, NOT THE WRITER. THERE IS NO NEED

TO SPECIFY "MED. SHOT," "THREE SHOT," "CHEST SHOT"

OR ANY OTHER DESIGNATIONS THAT ARE NOT TOTALLY

NECESSARY TO THE IMPACT AND IMAGE OF YOUR SCENE.)

-3-

FRED

In some scripts, the writer breaks

out the "video" and "audio" sections

① CU FRED   into two separate columns. This is

(Ready cam②)   not really necessary in television

(Ready Music)

1- Slow Z/I   drama, since you have enough room on

R/EFX   either side of the directions to

coordinate and put in appropriate

② WS BED   directorial markings. ←

This is the way a director might mark the script to indicate precise camera coverage and upcoming technical cues... The wide margin format allows the room for directorial notations.

(WHEN YOU END YOUR SCENE, TRY TO GO OUT ON A

REACTION OR A KEY PIECE OF VISUAL INFORMATION,

AND THEN YOU CAN...)

Here's how to indicate a switch to a totally different location and scene

                    CUT TO: ←

INT. HOTEL LOBBY--DAY ← *here's how to set up the new scene*

(AGAIN, YOU MUST DESCRIBE THE SET, DEFINE THE SHOT

VISUALLY FOR THE READER-PRODUCER-DIRECTOR, AND

DESCRIBE THE CHARACTERS. BE SURE TO STATE WHO

The new scene is described here

THEY ARE, WHAT THEY LOOK LIKE, AND WHAT THEY ARE

DOING.)

                 FRED

a small piece of character "business" or action might go in the stage directions above -- or here

(LIGHTING HIS CIGARETTE) ←

Dialogue, by the way, should be crisp

-4-

FRED (Cont'd)

and to the point. And don't worry

if it doesn't look gramatically

correct. People just don't talk that

way. They speak colloquially, you

know? So make your characters talk

like a real person.

LINDA

attitudes can be
suggested here

(TRYING TO HIDE HER JEALOUSY)

And don't forget that characters react

to everything they see and hear. Spoken

or not. This helps build credible

motivations and identifiable behavior

patterns.

Music or sound effects are
set up in a separate line of
stage directions

MUSIC UP: IF YOU HAVE <u>MUSIC</u> OR <u>SOUND EFFECTS</u>, THIS

IS HOW TO WRITE THEM IN.

LINDA (Cont'g)

If a character is
continuing dialogue
from above,
uninterrupted

I'd rather listen to the stereo,

wouldn't you?

(FRED GRINS).

here's how to write a reaction
without cutting to a CLOSE UP.

FADE OUT.

This is the
last direction
in any
script

or

FADE TO BLACK.

As you can see, the structure of the videotape script has several recognizable features: (1) every line is double-spaced; (2) every line is capitalized—except dialogue; (3) scene descriptions and stage directions are brief, and usually put within parentheses (this aspect varies from studio to studio); (4) the stage directions and dialogue are centered on the page, although some production companies shift those directions to the right or left (depending on whether the director is right-handed or left-handed). They might also reverse the capitalization system or discard the parentheses system. If you know the specific studio format, it's advisable to conform to those standards. If not, choose one style and stay consistent.

How to Write Stage Directions

In a videotape script stage directions are relatively brief. Compared to film, there is not much latitude for embellishing mood and atmosphere. This, for example, is the opening scene from a videotape script called "The New Little Rascals," a pilot project for Norman Lear's T.A.T. Communications Company. Note that the scene is relatively short and the stage directions are quite explicit. In addition, the stage directions are *not* in parentheses.

"GLUE'S COMPANY"

ACT ONE

SCENE I

INT. SCHOOLROOM

SPANKY SITS AT HIS DESK, GLUING TOGETHER A MODEL OF THE WRIGHT

BROTHERS' AIRPLANE. HE IS USING A LARGE SQUEEZE BOTTLE OF GLUE

WITH A DISTINCTIVE LABEL: "FUN-NEE GLUE. FAST, FAST, FAST!"

HE IS NOT BEING TOO CAREFUL; AS HE APPLIES GLUE TO THE PLANE,

WE SEE A LARGE DRIP RUN DOWN HIS SHIRT FRONT. AT A NEARBY DESK,

ALFALFA IS METICULOUSLY LINING UP SEVERAL ROWS OF PLASTIC INDIANS

AND OLD-WEST CAVALRY.

SPANKY

Jeez, this glue is fast! Look at this!

"GLUE'S COMPANY" CONTINUED

ALFALFA LOOKS. SPANKY TOUCHES A PIECE INTO PLACE ON THE PLANE
IT STICKS IMMEDIATELY, SOUNDLY.

                        ALFALFA

            Wow! Can I borrow that stuff?

                        SPANKY

            Sure, when I'm done. What're you

            working on?

                        ALFALFA
    (WITH A PROUD GESTURE TOWARD THE SOLDIERS AND INDIANS)

            It's "Custer's Last Stand!"

HIS HAND BRUSHES AGAINST A SOLDIER, WHICH FALLS AGAINST THE NEXT,
WHICH FALLS AGAINST THE NEXT. . . UNTIL WHOLE ARRANGEMENT HAS
FALLEN OVER LIKE SO MANY DOMINOES.

                        SPANKY

            Not any more, it isn't.

WITH A SHRUG, ALFALFA RISES, MOVES TOWARD THE DOOR.

                        ALFALFA

            Oh, well. No point setting 'em up until

            Jinx gets here with the diorama. See you.

                        SPANKY

            See you.

ALFALFA EXITS.

SPANKY APPLIES GLUE TO PLANE, GETTING SOME ON HIS HAND. HE
REACHES OVER WITH GLUEY HAND, PICKS UP PLANE WING. DECIDES
IT ISN'T READY YET, MOVES TO SET WING DOWN: IT WON'T GO. HE
TRIES AGAIN: WING IS STUCK TO HIS HAND.

                    SPANKY (cont'd)
        . . . huh?

HE SHAKES HAND VIOLENTLY; WING DOESN'T COME OFF.

STARING INTENTLY AT WING, HE PUTS ELBOWS ON DESK,

IDLY LAYING FREE HAND ATOP FUSELAGE. HE THINKS A

MOMENT, THEN SITS BACK WITH RESOLVE.

        This glue can't be all that--

HE GESTURES WITH WHAT WAS HIS FREE HAND; THE FUSELAGE

STICKS TO IT. HE DOES TAKE.

        Oh no!

HE SHAKES BOTH HANDS VIOLENTLY; NOTHING COMES LOOSE.

HE PULLS AT WING, THEN AT FUSELAGE; NOTHING. HIS EYE

FALLS ON THE GLUE BOTTLE

                    SPANKY (Cont'd)
        The bottle! The bottle'll say what

        to do!

USING WING AND FUSELAGE AS IF THEY WERE HANDS, HE

MANEUVERS BOTTLE SO HE CAN READ THE LABEL. HE READS

AVIDLY. . . AND HIS FACE FALLS.

        . . . the bottle says zero!

HE RISES, DETERMINED.

                    SPANKY (Cont'd)
        0-kay. I'm not gonna panic. I'm not

        gonna run around screaming for help.

LOOKING INTENTLY AT HIS HANDS, HE BEGINS TO PACE. HE BUMPS

INTO ALFALFA'S DESK, FALLS SPREADEAGLE, FACE DOWN ATOP THE

PLASTIC FIGURES.

"GLUE'S COMPANY" CONTINUED

<u>STOP TAPE</u>.

<u>RESUME ON</u>:

<u>ANOTHER ANGLE</u>:

SPANKY RISES FROM ALFALFA'S DESK: ALL BUT ONE OF THE SOLDIERS

AND INDIANS ARE NOW STUCK TO HIS SHIRT FRONT. HE TUGS HELPLESSLY

AT ONE OR TWO OF THEM, THEN LOOKS UP, EYES WIDE WITH ALARM.

SPANKY

Help! Help!

●   ●   ●

The whole scene takes place in one set—A SCHOOLROOM—which makes it easier to shoot, and inexpensive to produce. The writer suggests visual blocking and action, but doesn't overdirect with specific angles.

One device the writer employs is the STOP TAPE direction at the closing of the scene. He then resumes the action on ANOTHER ANGLE with SPANKY fully covered by plastic figures. When the sequence is edited together, it will look like SPANKY falls on the plastic figures, then gets right up from the desk with all the figures stuck to his shirt. The STOP TAPE direction allows time for such technical changes required on the set.

After the script is written, the writer reviews each scene to identify casting and location needs. That information is summarized in a Cast and Set sheet that is placed in the front of the script. This is the Cast and Set list from "The New Little Rascals" script:

"GLUE'S COMPANY"

<u>CAST</u>

ALFALFA

SPANKY

JINX

JO JO

FELIX

TURK

ISH

BELLADONNA

MR. SOPWORTH

POLICEMAN (OFFICER WITOWSKI)

SETS

INT. SCHOOLROOM

EXT. SCHOOL HOUSE (SIDE)

EXT. SCHOOL YARD

EXT. BUSINESS STREET

EXT. VACANT LOT

EXT. RESIDENTIAL STREET #1

EXT. RESIDENTIAL STREET #2

INT. BAG IT 'N BEAT IT

EXT. SPANKY'S HOUSE

The Variety Show Format

In the variety show genre, scenes are referred to as "segments," but the general wide-margin format stays the same. Even songs are double-spaced and centered on the page. Here's what a sample song segment looks like:

SEGMENT TWO: "What's the Sense"

(MERV HANDS JODY THE MICROPHONE AS THE LIGHTS BEGIN TO DIM)

(JODY GETS UP, TAKES THE MICROPHONE, AND DOES 'WHAT'S THE

SENSE'* SEGMENT)

JODY

(SINGING)

What's the sense of talking

If your talking ain't real talking

And if you don't mean anything you're sayin'?

What's the sense of meaning

If your meaning is deceiving

And your actions don't believe in what

  you're sayin'. . .

(CHORUS)

Pack your bags, leave me alone, just go

  away

Your   talk is golden but your feet are

  made of clay. . .

I'm stronger now than I was stronger

  yesterday.

JODY

(SINGING)

Mmm Mmm Mmm. . .

What's the sense of holdin',

If the love I hold is foldin'

And the spark that's left is blowin'

  in the wind?

What's the sense of pleading

If I'm pleading for self-pity and

If plastic smiles are painted on my friends?

(CHORUS)

Pack your bags, leave me alone, just

go away

Your talk is golden but your feet are

made of clay. . .

I'm stronger now than I was stronger

yesterday.

(APPLAUSE)

(JODY BOWS, GIVES THE MICROPHONE TO THE HOST, AND MAKES HER WAY

OVER TO THE PLATFORM SET.)

• • •

The Double-Column Format

A double-column format is sometimes used for documentary scripts, educational programs, commercials, and other projects requiring a running narrative. This form breaks the script into two columns—the left is for *video* or *picture;* the right is for *audio* or *sound*. Generally, every camera direction, scene description, and stage direction is capitalized. Only the dialogue remains in lower case letters.

The double-column format is supposed to provide a simultaneous sense of picture and sound. As an example, here is the opening sequence from a non-commercial television project called "The Magic Hearing Box." The script deals with the ramifications of hearing loss in children, and how they learn to cope with the situation.

*"What's the Sense?", music and lyrics by R. Blum; © 1980 Laurelton Music & Entertainment; All Rights Reserved.

Video	Audio
<u>FADE IN</u>:	SNEAK IN MUSIC:
WE SEE AN ALBUM PHOTO OF A SMILING BABY.	UNDER MUSIC, WE HEAR THE MUTED SOUNDS OF A BABY CRYING.
WE SEE A BABY'S RATTLE POKING OUT OF A CARDBOARD BOX.	THE SOUND OF A RATTLE, AND A BABY COOING.
A SPINNING TOP RESTS QUIETLY ON ITS SIDE.	WE HEAR A BABY BABBLING, CONTINUED FROM ABOVE.
A SCRATCHED PLASTIC FERRIS WHEEL SITS ON TOP OF A DRESSER.	THE SUSPENDED SOUNDS OF A MUSICAL LULLABY FROM SOME FARAWAY MUSIC BOX.
A RAGGEDY ANN DOLL SITS ON THE HEAD OF AN OVER-STUFFED LION.	WE HEAR A CHILD GIGGLE, PLAYING WITH HER TOYS.
A SMALL, SCRATCHED ROCKING HORSE.	THE SQUEAKING OF A ROCKING HORSE, A CHILD RIDING, LAUGHING.
<u>CUT TO</u> CLOSE UP-FRAMED PHOTO OF MELISSA. TEN YEARS OLD, A WIDE GRIN, A HAPPY FACE. SLOW ZOOM-IN TO ECU MELISSA, UNTIL PICTURE BECOMES GRAINY.	MOTHER (V.O.) Melissa was about two when we found out she had hearing problems. It was a hard thing for us to accept at first.

●   ●   ●

The actual format you select for your script depends strictly on the needs of the show you create. If it's in the dramatic vein, the wide-margin format is the most widely used. If your program is more narrative in structure, the double-column approach might be more suitable.

10

A Check-List for
Script Revision

Rewriting is a time-consuming process that can help make your script more competitive in the marketplace. With a certain degree of objectivity you can approach the story's pacing, the visual imagery, and the credibility of the characters and dialogue. The script can be analyzed for strengths and weaknesses on several important levels. Here is a check-list of some critical areas to question as you analyze the first draft of your work.

1) *Is the Script Visual?*

A script should make the best use of the television medium. As you read the draft, can you actually visualize the scene unfolding? Descriptions should be clear and cinematically interesting. Camera angles can be suggested, character actions amplified, locations sharply defined. As you spot problems in the draft, note in the margins that it may need more visual development.

2) *Is the Script Produceable?*

No matter how good the script, it won't be produced if it calls for $35 million worth of sets, period costumes, world-wide locations, hundred of stars, thousands of extras, and impossible camera shots. The script should be realistically conceived in terms of production requirements, locations, and casting needs.

3) *Is the Script Format Professional, and the Content Readable?*

Even the most powerful script can slip by the wayside if the format looks amateurish to a reader. If you have questions about script form, check the sample formats in this book as a guide. In addition, look at the clarity of writing in the script. Sometimes scene descriptions are too choppy, cluttered with information, or too repetitious. Smooth out the writing style for the most effective impact on the reader.

4) *Is the Story Focused and Well-Developed?*

Here you must examine the structure of the dramatic action points. Some scenes may lag, others may be redundant. As you read the script, assess the effectiveness of the plot sequences. If the story is unclear or erratic, it's time to "snip and tape." One sequence might work better at the beginning or end, which means reorganizing the entire story line, dropping scenes, adding new ones, polishing others.

5) *Is the Dramatic Conflict Strong and the Pacing Effective?*

The script should hold and build audience interest throughout each act. If the conflict is cleverly set up, and the stakes are high (ie, *sense of urgency* is great), audience involvement with the characters and conflicts increase. The pacing is most effective when scenes build upon each other in a careful, logical sequence of dramatic action.

6) *Is the Mood Accurately Conveyed?*

Each scene should help create the atmosphere of the show. If the descriptions are not vivid enough, take time to rewrite them. Don't settle for less than the most illustrative images of the place, action and characters.

7) *Are the Characters Likeable, Identifiable, and Consistently Developed?*

Be sure the characters are fully and credibly motivated. Are the interrelationships clearly drawn? If not, see if you can strengthen them through the *Method*-writer constructs, using super-objectives, through-line-of-action, intentions, motivations, sense of urgency, and moment-to-moment realities.

8) *Is the Dialogue Realistic and Sharply Defined?*

If the dialogue appears to be awkward in some places, check all the pertinent problems. Characters are unique individuals, and their dialogue should reflect that individuality. If a word is off, write *"b.w."* (find a "better word") in the margin, or write *"b.l."* (find a "better line") to correct the problem. It may seem like nit-picking, but don't let those little problems slip away. If your show reaches the air, those lines will make you cringe in living color.

● ● ●

Once all the points are addressed, and the major revisions are incorporated into the script, there's one more stop-check point. It's called the *polish.* Once more, go over the script with a fine-tooth comb. Be sure the story is focused, the characters are three-dimensional, dialogue is refined, action is visual, the mood is conveyed, and the pacing is effective. After all, this is the script that may eventually wind up in the archives of the Academy of TV Arts and Sciences—or at least in the hands of a reputable agent.

PART FOUR

MARKETING

11

How to Sell Your Project

What You Should Know Before Marketing

Marketing a script requires strategy, determination, and a realistic understanding of the industry. The marketplace is extremely competitive, and even the best projects written by established professionals might end up on the shelf. Still, an *excellent* original script—submitted to the right person at the right time—might suddenly break through all barriers. The key word is *excellent*. It makes no sense to submit a script unless you feel that it is in the most polished form (even then it will be subject to rewrites), and that it represents the highest calibre of your creative potential. One might think producers are inclined to see the masterpiece lurking behind a rough draft script. More likely, they'll focus on the weaknesses, compare it to top submissions, and generalize about the writer's talents. So, if you feel uncertain about the professional quality of a work, hold off submitting it. Your next work might show you off to better advantage.

How Many Copies of the Project are Needed.

Since unsolicited scripts tend to be lost or "misplaced" by production companies, it's a good idea to have a sufficient number of copies. The *minimum* number you will need is three—one for your files, one for submission, and one for inevitable rewrites. More realistically, you'll probably want additional copies for two or three producers, an agent or two, and your own reserve file for unanticipated submissions. Incidentally, fancy covers and title designs are totally unnecessary. Three inexpensive paper fasteners can be punched through the left hand margins of the manuscript. Scripts are usually photocopied to avoid the smudged look of carbons.

Script Registration

Any writer can register a story, treatment, series format, or script with the Writers Guild of America. The service was set up to help writers establish the completion dates of their work. It doesn't confer statutory rights, but it does supply evidence of authorship which is effective for ten years (and is renewable after that). If you want to register a project, send one copy along with the appropriate fee ($10 nonmembers; $4 members) to: Writers Guild of America Registration Service, 8955 Beverly Blvd., Los Angeles, California 90048.

You can also register dramatic or literary material with the U.S. Copyright Office—but most television writers rely on the Writers Guild. The Copyright Office is mainly used for book manuscripts, plays, music or lyrics, which the Writers Guild will not register. For appropriate copyright forms (covering dramatic compositions), write to: Register of Copyrights, Library of Congress, Washington, D.C. 20540.

The Release Form or Waiver

If you have an agent, there is no need to bother with release forms. But if you're going to submit a project without an agent, you'll have to send for a release form—or waiver—in advance. Most production companies will return your manuscript without it. The waiver states that you won't sue the production company and that the company has no obligations to you. That may seem unduly harsh, but consider the fact that millions of dollars are spent on fighting plagiarism suits, and that hundreds of ideas are being developed simultaneously and coincidentally by writers, studios, and networks.

The waiver is a form of self-protection for the producer who wants to avoid unwarranted legal action. But it also establishes a clear line of communication between the writer and producer. So rest assured, if legal action is warranted, it can be taken.

Writing a Cover Letter

When you prepare to send out your project, draft a cover letter that is addressed to a *person* at the studio, network, or production company. If you don't know who is in charge of program development, look it up in the trade papers, or call the studio receptionist. If she says, "Mr. So-and-So handles new projects," ask her to *spell* "Mr. So-and-So." That courtesy minimizes the chance of embarrassment, and maximizes the chance that the project will wind up at the right office.

The letter you write should sound professional. There's no need to offer apologies for being an unsold writer, or to suggest that the next draft will be ten times better than this one. If a cover letter starts off with apologies, what incentive is there to read the project?

Here's the tone a cover letter might have:

Dear _____

I've just completed a mini-series called FORTUNES, based on the book by Marian Sherry. I've negotiated all TV and film rights to the property, which is a dramatic adventure series about a family caught in the California Gold Rush. I think you'll find the project suitable for the mini-series genre. It's highly visual in production values and offers unusual opportunities for casting.

I look forward to your reactions. Thank you for your cooperation.

Sincerely,

The letter doesn't say I'm an unsold writer in the midwest or that Marian Sherry is my sister-in-law who let me have the rights for a handshake. Nor does it take the opposite route, aggressively asserting that it is the best project the studio will ever read. There's no need for such pretentions. The cover letter sets the stage in a simple and dignified manner. The project will have to speak for itself.

Where to Submit Your Project

Independent producers represent the widest span of marketing potential for the freelance writer. If one producer turns down an idea, there are many others who might still find it fresh and interesting. However, the smaller independent producer is not likely to have the financial resources to compete with the development monies available at the network or studio.

Production companies do have that bargaining power. The distinction between smaller independents and larger production companies is their relative financial stability and current competitive strength on the airwaves. Production companies form and dissolve according to the seasonal marketing trends and network purchases. The more successful production companies have become mini-studios in their own right, with a great number of programs on the air and in development. Some of the more recognizable entities are Q.M. Productions (Quinn Martin), M.T.M. Enterprises (Mary Tyler Moore), T.A.T. Communications

(Norman Lear), and Lorimar Productions (Lee Rich). (Addresses of selected production companies are listed in the *Appendix*.)

The major motion picture studios are in keen competition with production companies. Only six major studios have aggressive and viable television divisions: Columbia Pictures—TV; Paramount Pictures—TV; Metro-Goldwyn-Mayer (M.G.M.)—TV; 20th Century-Fox—TV; Universal—TV; and Warner Brothers—TV. They represent highly fertile ground for program development; strong deals can be negotiated for the right project.

At the top of the submission ladder is the network oligarchy: ABC, CBS, NBC. Once a project is submitted at this level, there's no turning back. If a project is "passed" (*i.e.*, turned down), it's too late to straddle down the ladder to independent producers. *Their* goal is to bring it back up to the networks (who in turn must sell to the sponsors).

A visual model of the writer's marketplace in network television is shown on the next page.

As the model shows, the closer the project comes to the network, the more limited the number of buyers. As the submission moves up the ladder, it faces stiffer competition and fewer alternatives. So you see that the marketplace is highly competitive, although not totally impenetrable. Your submission strategy will depend on knowing the marketplace trends and organizing a campaign to reach the most appropriate people and places.

How to Submit Your Project

There's no better way to stay on top of marketing trends and personnel changes than reading the trade papers—*Daily Variety* and *The Hollywood Reporter*. The trades reflect the daily pulse of the entertainment industry on the West Coast. Moreover, each paper offers a weekly compilation of production activities ("TV Production Chart," "Films in Production," etc.) which list companies, addresses, phone numbers, and producers for shows in work. A careful scrutiny of those lists will provide helpful clues to the interests and current activities of independent producers, production companies, and studios.

One of the most comprehensive marketing sources is *The Script writers' Marketplace*, a quarterly publication of the *Hollywood Reporter*, which identifies key contacts at major studios and production companies in the current TV season.

A similar resource is the "Television Market List" published regularly in the *Writers' Guild of America Newsletter*. It lists all current shows in production or pre-production, and identifies the story consultant or submission contact for each show. As in *The Scriptwriters' Marketplace*, it

Where to Submit Your Property

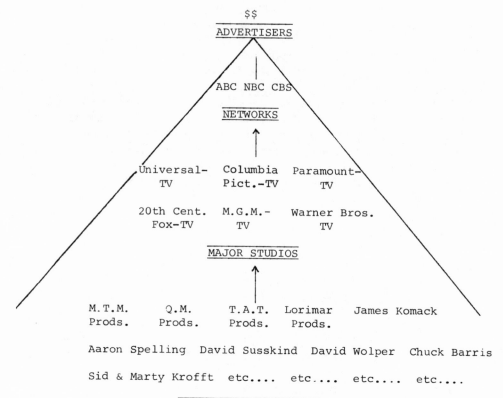

$$
ADVERTISERS

ABC NBC CBS

NETWORKS

Universal- Columbia Paramount-
TV Pict.-TV TV

20th Cent. M.G.M.- Warner Bros.
Fox-TV TV TV

MAJOR STUDIOS

M.T.M. Q.M. T.A.T. Lorimar James Komack
Prods. Prods. Prods. Prods.

Aaron Spelling David Susskind David Wolper Chuck Barris

Sid & Marty Krofft etc.... etc.... etc.... etc....

PRODUCTION COMPANIES

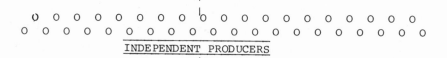

INDEPENDENT PRODUCERS

FREELANCE WRITERS

states whether or not a show is "open" for submissions, and who to contact for assignments. A careful reading of these and other publications can help bring you closer to making knowledgeable and practical decisions about marketing your own projects. (For a list of "Trade Publications and Periodicals of Interest to Writers," see the *Appendix*).

Submission Status Reports

In the network marketplace, you have a choice of *flooding the market* with a project (i.e., submitting it to a great number of sources at the same time) or *shopping it selectively* to a few individuals. The specific strategy depends on the needs of the marketplace at the time, and the strengths of your particular project. You should determine which producers and production companies are particularly interested in the type of project you've developed.

Marketing a television property requires time and patience. Each project needs an individual marketing strategy with independent files and records. It's helpful to keep a "Project Status Report," summarizing pertinent information about marketing contacts, dates, reactions, and follow-ups to each project. That information can be kept on 5 × 7 cards or on regular typing paper. This is one way it might be set up:

```
PROJECT STATUS REPORT
PROJECT TITLE:
DATE COMPLETED/REGISTERED:
SEND TO:        DATE MAILED:      RESPONSE:      FOLLOW-UP:
1.
2.
3.
4.
5.
```

Under the first column (*SEND TO*) you can pre-select names and addresses of producers, program development executives, agents who might be interested in your project. If the first person turns down the project, or doesn't respond in a reasonable period of time (4–6 weeks), send it to the next person on the list. This pre-selected listing provides you with a planned strategy for an erratic marketplace.

The second column (*DATE MAILED*) indicates when you forwarded—or *plan* to forward—the project to each person on the list.

In the next column (*RESPONSE*) you can summarize reactions received, e.g., "received letter from studio. They're not interested in this genre, but like my writing style. Asked to see more material."

The final column (*FOLLOW-UP*) leaves room for your initiatives, e.g., "if no word from studio, phone them"; "sent copy of another screenplay, per their request."

Project status reports can help keep track of submission strategies, problems, and solutions on a day-to-day basis.

Options, Contracts, and Pay Scales: What Happens if a Producer is Interested

If a producer is interested in a project he or she will propose a *deal, i.e.,* the basic terms for a contract. If you have no agent, now is the time to get one. *Any* agent will gladly close the deal for the standard 10% commission. An attorney would be equally effective, or if you have an appropriate background, you might want to close the deal yourself. The need for counsel depends on the complexity of the proposed deal, and the counter-proposals you wish to present.

On the basis of your discussions, a *Deal Memo* is drawn up which outlines the basic points of agreement—who owns what, for how long, for how much, with what credits, royalties, rights, and so on. The deal memo is binding, although certain points may be modified if both parties initial it. The *Contract* is based on the terms of the deal memo and is the formal legal document. If you're dealing with a producer who is a signatory to the Writers Guild (most established producers are), the contract will adhere to the terms of the Minimum Basic Agreement (M.B.A.) negotiated by the Writers Guild of America.

Here is a copy of the standard contract form for freelance film television writers:

STANDARD FORM FREELANCE FILM TELEVISION WRITER'S EMPLOYMENT CONTRACT.

Agreement entered into at _____, this_____ day of_____, 19_____ between_____, hereinafter called "Company" and _____, hereinafter called "Writer",

WITNESSETH:

1.   Company hereby employs the Writer to render services in the writing, composition, preparation and revision of the literary material described in subsection 2. hereof, hereinafter for convenience referred to as the "work". The Writer accepts such employment and agrees to render his services hereunder and devote his best talents, efforts and abilities in accordance with the instructions, control and directions of the Company.

2. **FORM OF WORK:**

( ) Plot outline (based on _____).

( ) Story (based on _____).

( ) Story and teleplay (based on_____).

( ) Teleplay (based on _____).

( ) Rewrite (of_____).

( ) Polish (of _____).

( ) Other material (described as _____).

3. **DELIVERY:**

If the Writer has agreed to complete and deliver the work, and/or any changes and revisions, within a certain period or periods of time, then such agreement will be expressed in this paragraph as follows:

4. **RIGHT TO OFFSET:**

With respect to Writer's warranties and indemnification agreement, the Company and the Writer agree that upon the presentation of any claim or the institution of any action involving a breach of warranty, the party receiving notice thereof will promptly notify the other party in regard thereto. Company agrees that the pendency of any such claim or action shall not relieve the Company of its obligation to pay the Writer any monies due hereunder, and the Company will not have the right to withhold such monies until it has sustained a loss or suffered an adverse judgment of decree by reason of such claim or action.

5. **COMPENSATION:**

As full compensation for all services to be rendered hereunder, the rights granted to the company with respect to the work, and the undertakings and agreements assumed by the Writers, and upon condition that the Writer shall fully perform such undertakings and agreements, Company will pay the Writer the following amounts:

a. Compensation for services $_____

b. Advance for television re-runs $_____

c. Advance for theatrical use $_____

No amounts may be inserted in b. or c. above unless the amount set forth in a. above is at least twice the applicable minimum compensation set forth in the Writers Guild of America Theatrical and Television Basic Agreement of 1977 (herein ''Basic Agreement'') for the type of services to be rendered hereunder.

If the assignment is for story and teleplay or teleplay the following amounts of the compensation set forth in a. above will be paid in accordance with the provisions of Article 13B of said Basic Agreement.

(1) $_____ following delivery of story.

(2) $_____ following delivery of first draft teleplay.

(3) $_____ following delivery of final draft teleplay.

In the event Writer receives screen credit as provided in Article 15B 13. of the Basic Agreement on the television film based on the above work and said film is exhibited theatrically, Company shall pay to the Writer the additional sum of $_____.

6.   MINIMUM BASIC AGREEMENT:

The parties acknowledge that this contract is subject to all of the terms and provisions of the Basic Agreement and to the extent that the terms and provisions of said Basic Agreement are more advantageous to Writer than the terms hereof, the terms of said Basic Agreement shall supersede and replace the less advantageous terms of this agreement. Writer is an employee as defined by said Basic Agreement and Company has the right to control and direct the services to be performed.

7.   GUILD MEMBERSHIP:

To the extent that it may be lawful for the Company to require the Writer to do so, Writer agrees to become and/or remain a member of Writers Guild of America in good standing as required by the provisions of said Basic Agreement. If Writer fails or refuses to become or remain a member of said Guild in good standing, as required in the preceding sentence, the Company shall have the right at any time thereafter to terminate this agreement with the Writer.

IN WITNESS WHEREOF, the parties hereto have duly executed this agreement on the day and year first above written.

By _____

Company

_____

Writer

(The foregoing Freelance Film Television Writer's Contract may contain any other provisions acceptable to both Writer and company and not less favorable to, inconsistent with or violative of any of the terms or provisions of the Basic Agreement above mentioned.)

• • •

A producer can either option your work, purchase it outright, or assign you to write new material. If the property is *optioned,* the producer pays for the right to shop it around (which means the project can be submitted by the producer to a third party, e.g., the network). During the option period, you can't submit the project to any one else. Typically, option money is relatively small; perhaps $1,500 or $2,500 for a six-month period. But the writer will be paid an additional sum of money if the producer elicits interest and moves the project forward. If the producer fails to exercise the option (*i.e.,* if the option expires), the rights revert back to the writer.

A *Step Deal* is the most common form of agreement between producers and freelance writers. It sets forth fees and commitments for story and teleplay in several phases. The first step is at the *story* stage. When the writer turns in a treatment, the producer pays for it—at least 30% of the total agreed upon compensation—but the producer does not have to assign that writer to do the script. If the writer *is* retained, the producer exercises the *first draft* option. When that draft of the script is turned in, the writer receives a minimum of 40% of the total agreed upon compensation. Now the producer has the final option— putting the writer to work on the *final draft.* Once that script is received, the writer is entitled to the balance of payment. The *Step Deal* is a form of protection for the producer who can respond to the quality of content, the inviolability of delivery dates, and the acceptability of the project to the networks. It also guarantees the writer that his or her work will be paid for, whether there is a cut-off or a go-ahead on the project.

What Do Writers Get Paid?

Television writers are covered by the Minimum Basic Agreement (*M.B.A.*) of the Writers Guild of America. The going rates for television and film are published in the *Schedule of Minimums: Writers Guild of America Theatrical and Television Basic Agreement* (available from the Writers Guild of America).

The table below outlines some of the minimums and going rates for specific writing services on network shows. New writers generally receive minimum while writers with more than two credits receive the going rate (or higher).

If a writer has not been previously employed in television, films, or dramatic radio, there is a reduced rate that can be used for "flat deals." That rate can be determined by contacting the Guild. If the script is produced, using the writer's material, the payment will automatically be adjusted upward to the full minimum.

SAMPLE W.G.A. MINIMUMS
(3/2/80 - 3/1/81)

A. New Series Presentations

Format for New Series $ 2,515

"Bible" for Multi-Part Series
    (complete presentation)   12,714

Each story line over 6   1,271

B. Plot Outlines
(narrative synopsis of story)

30 min.	605
60 min.	1,148
90 min.	1,697
120 min.	2,237

C. Stories and Teleplays

(Note: Minimums for Pilot Stories and Teleplays are 150%
of the applicable rates below.)

	*High Budget TV Film	Low Budget TV Film
Story		
30 min.	$ 1,330	$ 1,028
60 min.	2,417	1,945
90 min.	3,503	2,861
120 min.	4,591	3,779
Teleplay		
30 min.	$ 2,160	$ 1,664
60 min.	4,186	3,175
90 min.	6,210	4,689
120 min.	8,237	6,205

Story and Teleplay
(same writer is assigned to both, i.e.,
no options involved for teleplay. These
are called "bargain rates.")

30 min.	$ 3,323	$ 2,569
60 min.	6,043	4,865
90 min.	8,759	7,153
120 min.	11,179	9,447

Going Rates and Bonus
(additional compensation is payable to
a writer for story and teleplay of network primetime series. A bonus is
automatically paid to writers who have
written at least twice in the genre.)

	Going Rates	Bonus
30 min.	$ 4,718	$ 2,021
60 min.	6,065	3,369
90 min.	10,108	3,369
120 min.	12,128	4,718

D. Rewrites and Polishes

	High Budget TV Film	Low Budget TV Film
Rewrites		
30 min.	$ 1,308	$ 982
60 min.	2,476	1,872
90 min.	3,646	2,765
120 min.	4,816	3,656
Polishes		
30 min.	$ 653	$ 489
60 min.	1,238	937
90 min.	1,822	1,384
120 min.	2,407	1,829

*NOTE: High Budget TV Films are considered those in which negative
costs are equal or greater than these amounts:

30 min.	$27,500
60 min.	$52,250
90 min.	$92,000
120 min.	$125,000

Low Budget TV Films are considered those in which negative
costs are less than the amounts above.

●   ●   ●

There is also a fee structure worked out for rewrites and polishes
on scripts.
Variety programs have a different fee structure based on the
length of the show, the number of writers on staff, the numbers of

shows per week, the sketches written, and so on. Similarly, writers for quiz and audience participation shows are paid according to the weekly unit of programs, the questions, answers, and stunts.

As for residuals, the writer is guaranteed 100% of the going rate for the first "in season" rerun. A second rerun pays 50% of the applicable rate, while a third pays 40%. If the show runs beyond that, residuals are received in perpetuity on a sliding scale.

In the area of non-commercial television, the Guild reached a model agreement with KCET in Los Angeles. These are sample minimums under the freelance agreement for public television, assuming that the project is for national audiences. Some of the total minimums are higher for PBS because no residual payments are available under this agreement:

SAMPLE MINIMUMS--W.G.A.-KCET AGREEMENT

	3/2/80- 3/1/81	3/2/81- 7/1/81
A. National Dramatic Programs		
30 Minute		
Story	$ 1,330	$ 1,410
Teleplay	3,117	3,304
*Add'l Compensation	1,482	1,571
TOTAL	$ 5,929	$ 6,285
60 Minute		
Story	$ 2,417	$ 2,562
Teleplay	5,367	5,689
*Add'l Compensation	2,594	2,750
TOTAL	$10,378	$11,001
90 Minute		
Story	$ 3,504	$ 3,714
Teleplay	7,109	7,536
*Add'l Compensation	3,539	3,751
TOTAL	$14,152	$15,001

*This additional compensation is payable only if the teleplay is produced.

B. Documentary Programs		
60 Minute		
Story	$ 1,527	$ 1,619
Telescript	$ 4,423	$ 4,688
Story and Telescript	$ 5,439	$ 5,765

A Word About Credits and Arbitration

Screen credits literally equate to money in the bank. If a writer receives sole credit—WRITTEN BY—he or she is entitled to full residual payment as well as payment for story and teleplay. An additional CREATED BY credit entitles the writer to 100% of royalties every time the show airs (that can translate to thousand of dollars each week for a new series).

If a producer employs another writer to revise a project—which happens frequently—the credit problem is automatically referred to the Writers Guild for arbitration. All written materials are reviewed by Guild members who agree to review projects anonymously. It's their job to decide who is entitled to what credit. If the final credit is sole story or teleplay (STORY BY or TELEPLAY BY), the residuals will be based on that contribution alone. If a credit is shared with another writer (STORY BY "A" AND "B"), so are the residual checks that come in the mail.

The issue of television credits is so important and complex that twelve pages of legal definitions and regulations are included in the Writers Guild *M.B.A.* In an effort to stay on top of credit problems, the Guild requires the production company to send a *Notice of Tentative Writing Credits* to Writers Guild headquarters, and to all participating writers on a show. If a writer protests the credits for any reason, the project automatically goes into the arbitration process.

This is the type of notice a writer might receive.

NOTICE OF TENTATIVE WRITING CREDITS

TO: Writers Guild of America, West, Inc. 8955 Beverly Boulevard, Los Angeles, California 90048 and Participating Writers

NAMES OF PARTICIPATING WRITERS   ADDRESS

_____   _____

_____   _____

Title of Episode: _____ Production #_____
                  (indicate if pilot)

Series Title: _____

Producing Company: _____

Executive Producer: _____

Producer: _____ Assoc. Producer: _____

Director: _____ Story Editor (or Consultant): _____

Other Production Executives, if Participating Writers _____

Writing credits on this episode are tentatively determined as follows:

ON SCREEN:

Source material credit ON THIS EPISODE (On separate card, unless otherwise indicated) if any:

Continuing source material or Created By credit APPEARING ON ALL EPISODES OF SERIES (on separate card, unless otherwise indicated) if any:

The above tentative credits will become final unless a protest or request to read the final script is communicated to the undersigned not later than 6:00 P.M. _____.

_____ BY: _____

How Do You Join the Writers Guild?

The Writers Guild of America protects writers' rights, and establishes minimum acceptable arrangements for fees, royalties, credits, and so on. You are eligible to join the Guild as soon as you sell your first project to a signatory company (one who has signed an agreement with the Guild). A copy of your contract is automatically filed and you will then be invited to join the membership. Before you sell the next project, you *have* to be a member of the Guild; otherwise, no signatory company can hire you.

The one-time membership fee is $500. In addition, 1% of yearly earnings as a writer (or $10 quarterly if you earn less than $1,000 as a writer).

How To Get an Agent

A good agent is one with a respectable track record, a prestigious list of clients, and a reputation for fairness in the industry. There is no magical list of good agents, although the Writers Guild does publish a list of agents who are franchised by the Guild. (For a list of agents who indicated they will read new material, see the *Appendix*). If you have no agent representing you, it's difficult to get projects considered by major producers.

One of the best ways to make headway is to submit your work to an agent who already represents a friend, a professor, a long-lost uncle in the industry. If you are recommended by someone known to the agency, it makes you less of an unknown commodity. If you have no contact, the quest for representation can still be handled effectively through the concept of marketing strategy. Work up a list of possible agents for your project, and prioritize them in your submission status file. You might send the project to one top agency for consideration, or to a select number of agencies at the same time. There is nothing wrong with a limited organized campaign which seeks representation for your project.

A brief cover letter might introduce you as a freelancer looking for representation on a specific project. If you don't get a response within six to eight weeks, you can follow up with a phone call or letter, and submit the project to the next agent on your list. Don't be discouraged if you get no response at first; just keep the project active in the field. If the script or presentation is good enough, you might eventually wind up with some positive and encouraging feedback from the agency.

If an agent is interested in your work, he or she will ask to represent it in the marketplace. If the work sells, the agent is entitled to 10% commission for closing the deal. If the work elicits interest but no sale, you have at least widened your contacts considerably for the next project.

Large and Small Agencies

The larger agencies—William Morris Agency, Inc., and International Creative Management (I.C.M.)—are virtually impenetrable to new writers. These agencies have a long list of clients in every field from variety and concerts to film, television, and the legitimate stage. They handle writers, producers, directors, actors, and even production companies. For that reason, a major agency can *package* top clients into a new project with a massive price tag attached. If the package is attractive enough, the script may sell at a very lucrative price for the writer.

The *package* is a strong way to present a new series presentation or script, but it is not without its drawbacks. The process may take as long as three or four months to set up, and may stretch out some additional months before getting a reading from the network. The most erratic aspect of packaging is the marketplace response. An entire deal can be blown if a key executive dislikes *any* of the elements attached. If one actor is preferred to another, or if the director is disliked by the executive's wife, months of waiting can explode into fragments of frustration. The project may never get off the ground.

The larger agencies offer an umbrella of power and prestige, but that elusive status is seriously undermined by the sheer size of the agency itself. Many clients inevitably feel lost in an over-crowded stable, and newcomers can hardly break into that race. In contrast, a smaller literary agency might provide more personalized service, and might be more open to the work of new talent. If you're going to seek representation, the smaller agency is the likely place to go. But don't be fooled by the label "small." Many of these agencies are exceptionally strong and have deliberately limited their client roster to the cream of the crop. In fact, many smaller agents have defected from executive positions at the major agencies. So you'll have to convince them you're the greatest writer since Shakespeare came on the scene—and that your works are even more saleable.

How do you prove that you have the talent to be a star talent? It's all in the writing. If your projects look professional, creative, and stylistically effective, you're on the right track. Indeed, you can call yourself a writer. If the artistic content is also marketable and you back it up with determination and know-how, you might just become a *selling* writer.

And that is the "bottom line" for success in the television industry.

PART FIVE

APPENDIX:

WHERE TO GO NEXT

Networks, Studios, and
Selected Production Companies

(*Note:* New submissions should be addressed to the Head of Program Development, and should be submitted through an agent, if possible.)

NETWORKS:

ABC-TV

2040 Ave. of the Stars		1330 Ave. of the Americas
Century City, CA 90067	or	New York, NY 10019
(213) 553-2000		(212) 581-7777

CBS-TV

7800 Beverly Blvd.		51 W. 52nd St.
Los Angeles, CA 90036	or	New York, NY 10019
(213) 852-2532		(212) 975-4321

NBC-TV

3000 W. Alameda		30 Rockefeller Plaza
Burbank, CA 91523	or	New York, NY 10020
(213) 845-7000		(212) 664-4444

MAJOR STUDIOS:

Columbia Pictures-TV
3000 Colgems Square
Burbank, CA 91505
(213) 843-6000

M.G.M.-TV
10202 W. Washington Blvd.
Culver City, CA 90230
(213) 836-3000

Paramount Pictures-TV
5451 Marathon St.
Los Angeles, CA 90038
(213) 468-5000

Universal Studios-TV
100 Universal City Plaza
Universal City, CA 91608
(213) 985-4321

20th Century Fox-TV
10201 W. Pico Blvd.
Los Angeles, CA 90064
(213) 277-2211

Warner Bros. TV
4000 Warner Blvd.
Burbank, CA 91522
(213) 843-6000

SELECTED INDEPENDENT PRODUCTION COMPANIES:

Bob Banner Productions
132 S. Rodeo Dr.
Beverly Hills, CA 90212
(213) 273-6923

Chuck Barris Productions
6430 Sunset Blvd.
Los Angeles, CA 90028
(213) 469-9080

Douglas C. Cramer Productions
10201 W. Pico Blvd.
Los Angeles, CA 90064
(213) 277-2211

Four D Productions (Danny Arnold)
1313 N. Vine St.
Los Angeles, CA 90028
(213) 663-3311

Walt Disney Productions
500 S. Buena Vista St.
Burbank, CA 91521
(213) 845-3141

EMI Productions (Roger Gimbel)
4024 Radford Ave.
Studio City, CA 91604
(213) 760-5000

Filmways TV Productions
1800 Century Park E.
Los Angeles, CA 90067
(213) 552-1133

Fries Productions (Charles Fries)
4024 Radford Ave.
Studio City, CA 91604
(213) 760-5000

Goodson-Todman Productions
6430 Sunset Blvd.
Los Angeles, CA 90028
(213) 464-4300

Henry Jaffe Enterprises
8321 Beverly Blvd.
Los Angeles, CA 90048
(213) 651-5340

James Komack Company
4151 Prospect Ave.
Los Angeles, CA 90027
(213) 663-3311

Sid and Marty Krofft Productions
7200 Vineland Ave.
Sun Valley, CA 91352
(213) 875-3250

Landsburg Productions (Alan
    Landsburg)
110 N. Doheny Dr.
Beverly Hills, CA
(213) 273-7400

Lorimar Productions (Lee Rich)
4000 Warner Blvd.
Burbank, CA 91522
(213) 843-6000

Marble Arch Productions
4024 Radford Ave.
Studio City, Calif. 91604
(213) 760-5000

M.T.M. Enterprises (Mary Tyler
   Moore, Grant Tinker)
4024 Radford Ave.
Studio City, CA 91604
(213) 760-5000

QM Productions (Quinn Martin)
1041 N. Formosa Ave.
Los Angeles, CA 90046
(213) 650-2500

Aaron Spelling Productions
10201 W. Pico Blvd.
Los Angeles, CA 90064
(213) 277-2211

David Susskind
747 3rd Ave.
New York, NY 10017
(212) 753-1030

T.A.T. Communications/Tandem
   Productions (Norman Lear)
5752 Sunset Blvd.
Los Angeles, CA 90028
(213) 462-7111

Time-Life Television
1041 N. Formosa Ave.
Los Angeles, CA 90046
(213) 650-2454

Titus Productions (Herb Brodkin)
211 E. 51st St.
New York, NY 10022
(212) 753-6460

Tomorrow Entertainment, Inc.
1041 N. Formosa
Los Angeles, Calif. 90046
(213) 851-4896

Ivan Tors Films, Inc.
942 Seward
Los Angeles, CA 90038
(213) 465-2805

David Wolper Productions
Warner Bros. TV
4000 Warner Blvd.
Burbank, CA 91522
(213) 843-6000

Federal Agencies, Private Foundations, and Public Television Associations

AGENCIES AND FOUNDATIONS

American Film Institute (AFI)
JFK Center for the Performing Arts
Washington, D. C. 20566
(202) 828-4000

AFI Center for Advanced Film Study
501 Doheny Rd.
Beverly Hills, CA 90210
(213) 278-8777

Carnegie Commission
1270 6th Ave.
New York, NY 10020
(212) 245-2700

Center for Arts Information
80 Centre St.
New York, NY 10013
(212) 488-2646

Children's Television Workshop
   (CTW)
1 Lincoln Plaza
New York, NY 10023
(212) 595-3456

Corporation for Public Broadcasting
   (CPB)
1111 Sixteenth St., N. W.

Washington, D. C. 20036
(202) 293-6160

The Film Fund
80 E. 11th St.
Suite 647
New York, NY 10003
(212) 475-3720

Ford Foundation
Office of Communications
320 E. 43rd St.
New York, NY
(212) 573-5000

The Foundation Center
888 7th Ave.
New York, NY 10019
(212) 489-8610

The Grantsmanship Center
1015 West Olympic Blvd.
Los Angeles, CA 90015
(213) 485-9094

John Simon Guggenheim Memorial
   Foundation
90 Park Ave.
New York, NY 10016
(212) 687-4470

John and Mary R. Markle Foundation
50 Rockefeller Plaza
New York, NY 10020
(212) 265-2795

National Association of Educational
  Broadcasters (NAEB)
1346 Connecticut Ave., N. W.
Washington, D. C. 20036
(202) 785-1100

National Endowment for the Arts
  (NEA)
Media Arts Program
2401 E Street, N. W.
Washington, D. C. 20506
(202) 634-6300
(Note: As of late 1981, NEA is located
  at Old Federal Post Office Bldg.,
  Washington, D. C.)

National Endowment for the
  Humanities (NEH)
Division of Public Programs—Media
806 15th St., N.W.
Washington, D. C. 20506
(202) 724-0318
(Note: As of late 1981, NEH is lo-
  cated at Old Federal Post Office
  Bldg., Washington, D. C.)

National Institute of Education (NIE)
1200 Nineteenth St., N. W.
Washington, D. C. 20208
(202) 254-6050

National Public Radio (NPR)
2025 M St., N. W.
Washington, D. C. 20036
(202) 785-5400

U.S. Office of Education
Dep't. of Education
330 Independence Ave., S. W.
Washington, D. C. 20201
(202) 655-4000

Public Broadcasting System (PBS)
475 L'Enfant Plaza, S. W.
Washington, D. C. 20024
(204) 488-5084

Rockefeller Foundation
Humanities Program
1133 Avenue of Americas
New York, NY 10036
(212) 265-8100

WNET/13 Television Laboratory
Independent Documentary Fund
356 West 58th St.
New York, NY 10019
(212) 560-3190

REGIONAL PUBLIC BROADCASTING NETWORKS

Central Educational Network
5400 N. St. Louis Ave.
Chicago, IL 60625
(312) 463-3040

Eastern Educational Network (EEN)
131 Clarendon St.
Boston, MA 02116
(617) 247-0470

Pacific Mountain Network
Suite 50-B, Diamond Hill
2480 W. 26th Ave.

Denver, CO 80211
(303) 455-7161

Southern Educational
  Communications Assn. (SECA)
P.O. Box 5966
Columbia, SC 29250
(803) 799-5517

Western Educational Society for
  Telecommunications (WEST)
Radio-TV Center
U. of Nevada
Reno, NV 89557
(702) 784-6591

Professional Guilds, Associations, and Trade Unions

Academy of Motion Picture Arts and
    Sciences
8949 Wilshire Blvd.
Beverly Hills, CA 90211
(213) 278-8900

Academy of TV Arts and Sciences
    (Hollywood)
6363 Sunset Blvd.
Suite 711
Hollywood, CA 90028
(213) 465-1137

Actors' Equity Association
1500 Broadway
New York, NY 10036
(213) 869-9530

American Federation of Television
    and Radio Artists (AFTRA)
1717 N. Highland
Hollywood, CA 90028
(213) 461-8111

American Film Institute (AFI)
JFK Center for Performing Arts
Washington, D. C. 20506
(202) 828-4000

American Guild of Variety Artists
    (AGVA)
1540 Broadway
New York, NY 10036
(212) 765-0800

American Women in Radio and
    Television, Inc. (AWRT)
1321 Connecticut Ave., N. W.
Washington, D. C. 20036
(202) 296-0009

Association of Motion Picture and TV
    Producers, Inc. (AMPTP)
8480 Beverly Blvd.
Los Angeles, CA 90048
(213) 653-2200

Caucus for Producers, Writers, &
    Directors
760 N. La Cienega Blvd.
Los Angeles, Calif. 90069
(213) 652-0222

Composers and Lyricists Guild of
    America, Inc.
6565 Sunset Blvd.
Hollywood, CA 90028
(213) 462-6068

159

Directors Guild of America, Inc.
7950 Sunset Blvd.
Hollywood, CA 90046
(213) 656-1220

International Radio and TV Society
420 Lexington Ave.
New York, NY 10017
(212) 532-4546

National Academy of TV Arts and
    Sciences
110 W. 57th St.
New York, NY 10019
(212) 765-2450

National Association of Broadcasters
    (NAB)
1771 N Street, N. W.
Washington, D. C. 20036
(202) 293-3500

PEN (Poets, Playwrights, Essayists,
    Editors, and Novelists)
American Center
156 Fifth Ave.
New York, NY 10010
(212) 255-1977

Producers Guild of America
8201 Beverly Blvd.
Los Angeles, CA 90048
(213) 651-0084

Screen Actors Guild (SAG)
7750 Sunset Blvd.
Hollywood, CA 90046
(213) 876-3030

Writers Guild of America, East, Inc.
22 West 48th St.
New York, NY 10036
(212) 575-5060

Writers Guild of America, West, Inc.
8955 Beverly Blvd.
Los Angeles, CA 90048
(213) 550-1000

Trade Publications and Periodicals of Interest to Writers

Broadcasting (weekly)
1735 DeSales St., N.W.
Washington, D. C. 20036
(202) 638-1022

Daily Variety (daily)
1400 N. Cahuenga Blvd.
Hollywood, CA 90028
(213) 469-1141

Editor and Publisher (weekly)
850 Third Ave.
New York, NY 10022
(212) 752-7050

Emmy (quarterly)
Academy of TV Arts and Sciences
6363 Sunset Blvd., Suite 711
Hollywood, CA 90028
(213) 465-1137

Fade In (quarterly)
Writers Guild of America West, Inc.
8955 Beverly Blvd.
Los Angeles, CA 90048
(213) 550-1000

Grants and Awards Available to American Writers (annual)
P.E.N.
American Center
156 Fifth Ave.
New York, NY 10010
(212) 255-1977

The Hollywood Reporter (daily)
6715 Sunset Blvd.
Hollywood, CA 90028
(213) 464-7411

Journal of Broadcasting (quarterly)
Department of Radio TV Film
Temple University
Philadelphia, PA 19122
(215) 787-8432

Media Report to Women (monthly)
3306 Ross Place, N.W.
Washington, D.C. 20008
(202) 363-0812

PACT Sheet (biweekly)
People and Careers in
    Telecommunication
NAEB
1346 Connecticut Ave, N.W.
Washington, D.C. 20036
(202) 785-1100

The Scriptwriters' Marketplace
    (quarterly)
The Hollywood Reporter
6715 Sunset Blvd.
Hollywood, CA 90028
(213) 464-7411

Television Quarterly (quarterly)
National Academy of TV Arts &
    Sciences
110 W. 57th St.
New York, NY 10019
(212) 765-2450

Variety (weekly)
154 West 46th St.
New York, NY 10036
(212) 582-2700

WGAW Newsletter (monthly)
Writers Guild of America West
8955 Beverly Blvd.
Los Angeles, CA 90048
(213) 550-1000

The Writer (monthly)
8 Arlington St.
Boston, MA 02116

Writer's Digest (monthly)
9933 Alliance Rd.
Cincinnati, OH 45242
(513) 984-0717

Writers Market (annual)
9933 Alliance Rd.
Cincinnati, OH 45242
(513) 984-0717

The Writer's Yearbook
9933 Alliance Rd.
Cincinnati, OH 45242
(513) 984-0717

Literary Agents Who May Consider Material from New Writers

The following agencies subscribed to the W.G.A.—Artists Managers' Basic Agreement, and indicated they will consider material from new writers. However, the Writers Guild has received a number of complaints from new writers. Even though the intent has been expressed, many agents are not able to afford time to read that material. Still, the list is provided to offer some sense of the smaller agencies that handle writer clients.

For an up-to-date listing of all *agencies that have subscribed to the W.G.A.—Artists Managers' Basic Agreement, contact the Writers Guild of America, West (8955 Beverly Blvd., Los Angeles, CA 90048).*

The Guild suggests that you contact the agency by letter or phone, detailing professional and/or academic credentials, and describing the nature of the project. If the agency expresses interest in seeing the manuscript, a stamped and self-addressed envelope (S.A.S.E.) should be enclosed.

(**indicates the agency will consider material from new writers only as a result of references from people known to the agency.)

Act 48 Management
1501 Broadway #1713
New York, NY 10036
(212) 354-4250

**Adams, Ray & Rosenberg
9200 Sunset Blvd.
Los Angeles, CA 90060
(213) 278-3000

Agency for Artists
9200 Sunset Blvd., #531
Los Angeles, CA 90060
(213) 278-6243

Barr/Wilder & Associates
8721 Sunset Blvd., #205
Los Angeles, CA 90060
(213) 652-7994

Bloom, Harry & Associates
9460 Wilshire Blvd., #425
Beverly Hills, CA 90212
(213) 550-8087

**Brady, Christina Agency
11818 Wilshire Blvd.
Los Angeles, CA 90025
(213) 473-2708

Brebner Agencies, Inc.
161 Berry Street
San Francisco, CA 94107
(415) 495-6700

Calder Agency, The
8749 Sunset Blvd.
Los Angeles, CA 90069
(213) 652-3380

Carter, Nancy, Agency Inc., The
1801 Ave. of the Stars, #640
Los Angeles, CA 90067
(213) 277-2683

CineScribe (Division of
    CineFemme)
P.O. Box 140337
Dallas, TX 75214
(214) 823-2740

Connell, Polly & Associates
4605 Lankershim Blvd.,
No. Hollywood, CA 91602
(213) 985-6266

De Lauer, Marjel
8961 Sunset Blvd.

Los Angeles, CA 90060
(213) 273-1133

**Diamond Artists Ltd.
9200 Sunset Blvd., #909
Los Angeles, CA 90060
(213) 278-8146

Felber, William Agency
2126 Cahuenga Blvd.
Hollywood, CA 90028
(213) 466-7629

Ferrell, Carol Agency
6331 Hollywood Blvd.
Hollywood, CA 90028
(213) 466-8311

Gault Agency
610 W. Main Street
Santa Maria, CA 93454
(805) 925-0547

Gibson, J. Carter Agency
9000 Sunset Blvd.
Los Angeles, CA 90060
(213) 274-8813

Goldfarb/Lewis Agency
8733 Sunset Blvd.
Los Angeles, CA 90069
(213) 659-5955

Green, Ivan Agency, The
1888 Century Park E., #908
Los Angeles, CA 90067
(213) 277-1541

**Halsey, Reece Agency
8733 Sunset Blvd.
Los Angeles, CA 90060
(213) 652-2409

Harvey & Hutto, Inc.
110 W. 57th St.,
New York, NY 10019
(212) 581-5610

Helton, Lorris Agency, The
8961 Sunset Blvd., #B
Los Angeles, CA 90060
(213) 273-6012

Irwin, Lou Inc. Agency
9901 Durant Dr.,
Beverly Hills, CA 90212
(213) 553-4775

Jackinson, Alex Literary Agency
55 W. 42nd St.
New York, NY 10036
(212) 563-0156

J. F. Images, Inc.
1776 S. Jackson St., Suite 702
Denver, CO 80213
(303) 758-7777

**Karlin, Larry
9200 Sunset Blvd.
Los Angeles, CA 90060
(213) 550-0570

King, Archer, Ltd.
777 Seventh Ave.
New York, NY 10019
(212) 581-8513

Kingsley Corporation, The
122D E. Center St.
Manchester, CT 06040
(203) 646-2597

Kozak, Otto R.
Literary & Motion Picture Agency
1089 West Park Ave.
Long Beach, NY 11561
(516) 889-4370

Lovell & Associates
8732 Sunset Blvd.
Los Angeles, CA 90060
(213) 659-8140

Markson, Raya Literary Agency
1888 Century Park E.

Los Angeles, CA 90067
(213) 552-2083

McClendon, Ernestine Enterprises,
    Inc.
8440 Sunset Blvd.
Los Angeles, CA 90060
(213) 654-4425

Memminger Agency, The
12069 Ventura Place
Studio City, CA 91604
(213) 980-4449

Miller, Michael McAndrews
163 E. 36th Street (PH)
New York, NY 10016
(212) 889-0503

Oscard, Fifi Associates, Inc.
19 W. 44th St.
New York, NY 10022
(212) 764-1100

Pagama Productions, Inc.
2186 Rawhide Street
Las Vegas, NV 89119
(702) 736-6303

Rifkin-David
9301 Wilshire Blvd., #306
Beverly Hills, CA 90210
(213) 550-0359

Robards, Bill Agency
4421 Riverside Drive
Toluca Lake, CA 91505
(213) 845-8547

Rosemary Management
11520 San Vicente Blvd.
Los Angeles, CA 90040
(213) 826-3453

SBK Associates
11 Chamberlain
Waltham, MA 02154
(617) 894-4037

Schuster-Dowdell Organization,
    The
P.O. Box 2
Valhalla, NY 10595
(914) 761-3106

Schwartz, Don & Associates, Inc.
8721 Sunset Blvd.
Los Angeles, CA 90069
(213) 657-8910

Shapiro, Susan
Box 626
New York, NY 10028
(212) 860-3996

Shapiro-Lichtman, Inc.
9200 Sunset Blvd.
Los Angeles, CA 90069
(213) 550-1020

Sherman & Associates
9507 Santa Monica Blvd.
Hollywood, CA 90210
(213) 273-8840

Soloway, Arnold Associates
118 S. Beverly Dr.
Beverly Hills, CA 90212
(213) 550-1300

Sugho, Larry Agency
1017 N. La Cienega Blvd.
Los Angeles, CA 90060
(213) 657-1450

**Swanson, H. N. Inc.
8523 Sunset Blvd.
Los Angeles, CA 90060
(213) 652-5385

Trejos & Trejos Literary Agency
18235 Avalon Blvd.
Carson, CA 90746
(213) 538-2945

TVR
P.O. Box 11574
Philadelphia, PA 19116
(215) 698-8170

Writers West Unlimited
1888 Century Park E.
Los Angeles, CA 90067
(213) 556-3465

**Weir, Ava
c/o Sterlyn International
Properties & Filmwork, Inc.
880 Fifth Ave.
New York, NY 10021
(212) 472-2814

Universities and Colleges Offering Courses in Film/TV Writing

The following list of universities and colleges was compiled by the research division of AFI, and was published in the *AFI Guide to College Courses in Film and Television, 6th edition*. It is reprinted here in modified form (by state) with the permission of the American Film Institute, J.F.K. Center for Performing Arts, Washington, D.C. In addition, some other schools, identified in a national survey of writing courses have been included.

If you are interested in learning more about the writing programs, contact the appropriate department head and ask about the school's writing emphasis (fiction, documentary, educational). You might also inquire about the number of courses available on the graduate and undergraduate level, and the professional credentials of the faculty. Moreover, ask about the prior success of students in the television-film marketplace. Some schools are much more successful than others in the placement of scripts and writers in the marketplace.

ALABAMA
Spring Hill College
University of Alabama

ALASKA
University of Alaska

ARIZONA
Arizona State University
University of Arizona

ARKANSAS
University of Arkansas, Fayetteville
University of Central Arkansas

CALIFORNIA
Antioch College/West
Art Center College of Design
California Institute of the Arts
California State College, Dominguez
   Hills

California State Polytechnic University, Pomona
California State University, Chico
California State University, Fresno
California State University, Fullerton
California State University, Long Beach
California State University, Los Angeles
California State University, Northridge
California State University, Sacramento
College of San Mateo
College of the Desert
Columbia College/California
Contra Costa College
Cosunmes River College
Diablo Valley College
Grossmont College
Humboldt State University
Loma Linda University
Lone Mountain College
Long Beach City College
Los Angeles City College
Los Angeles Pierce College
Loyola Marymount University
Merced College
Modesto Junior College
Palomar College
Pasadena City College
Pitzer College
Saddleback College
San Diego City College
San Diego State University
San Francisco State University
San Jose State University
Santa Monica College
Solano Community College
Stanford University
University of California, Irvine
University of California, Los Angeles
University of California, Santa Barbara
University of California, Santa Cruz
University of San Francisco
University of Southern California

COLORADO
Colorado State University
Regis College
University of Denver

CONNECTICUT
Fairfield University
University of Bridgeport
University of Connecticut, Storrs
University of New Haven
Yale University

DISTRICT OF COLUMBIA (D.C.)
Howard University
Mount Vernon College
University of the District of Columbia, Mount Vernon Square Campus

FLORIDA
Florida Technological University
Nova University
Pensacola Junior College
University of Florida
University of Miami
University of South Florida

GEORGIA
Georgia Southern College
University of Georgia
Valdosta State College

IDAHO
University of Idaho

ILLINOIS
Columbia College/Illinois
Concordia Teachers College
Governors State University
Illinois State University
Northern Illinois University
Northwestern University
Southern Illinois University, Carbondale
Southern Illinois University, Edwardsville
University of Illinois, Urbana-Champaign
Wheaton College

INDIANA
Purdue University
Ball State University
Butler University
Indiana University, Bloomington
University of Evansville
Vincennes University

IOWA
Buena Vista College
Clarke College
Drake University
Iowa State University
University of Iowa

KANSAS
Bethany College
Fort Hays State University
Kansas State University
Washburn University

KENTUCKY
Eastern Kentucky University
Henderson Community College,
    University of Kentucky
Kentucky Wesleyan College
Paducah Community College

LOUISIANA
Northwestern State University
University of New Orleans
University of Southwestern Louisiana

MAINE
University of Maine, Orono

MARYLAND
Antioch College
College of Notre Dame
Community College of Baltimore
Frostburg State College
Salisbury State College
Towson State College
University of Maryland, Baltimore
    County
University of Maryland, College Park

MASSACHUSETTS
Assumption College
Boston College

Boston University
Mount Wachusett Community
    College
Springfield Technical Community
    College
Suffolk University
Worcester State College

MICHIGAN
Central Michigan University
Eastern Michigan University
Grand Valley State Colleges, William
    James College
Lansing Community College
Northern Michigan University
University of Detroit
University of Michigan, Ann Arbor
Wayne State University
Western Michigan University

MINNESOTA
Carleton College
College of St. Catherine
College of St. Scholastica
College of St. Thomas
Film in the Cities
St. Cloud State University
St. Mary's College/Minnesota
University of Minnesota, Minneapo-
    lis/St. Paul
Winona State University

MISSISSIPPI
Mississippi State College
University of Mississippi
University of Southern Mississippi

MISSOURI
Central Missouri State University
Lindenwood Colleges
University of Missouri-Columbia
University of Missouri-Kansas City
St. Louis Community College at
    Florissant Valley

MONTANA
Miles Community College
Montana State University

NEBRASKA
University of Nebraska, Lincoln

NEVADA
University of Nevada, Las Vegas
University of Nevada, Reno

NEW HAMPSHIRE
Dartmouth College
University of New Hampshire

NEW JERSEY
Fairleigh Dickinson University-
    Madison
Glassboro State College
Jersey City State College
Montclair State College
Ramapo College of New Jersey
Seton Hall University
Stockton State College
William Paterson College of New
    Jersey

NEW YORK
Adelphi University
Bard College
City University of New York,
    Brooklyn College
City University of New York, City
    College
City University of New York, Hunter
    College
City University of New York, Lehman
    College
City University of New York, Queens
    College
College of Mount Saint Vincent
Columbia University
C.W. Post Center of Long Island
    University
Dowling College
Elizabeth Seton College
Fordham University
Hobart and William Smith Colleges
Ithaca College
New School for Social Research
New York University
Rochester Institute of Technology
The School of Visual Arts
St. Bonaventure University

State University of New York College
    at New Paltz
Syracuse University
Vassar College

NORTH CAROLINA
East Carolina University
North Carolina Agricultural and
    Technical State University
Shaw University
University of North Carolina at
    Chapel Hill
Western Carolina University

NORTH DAKOTA
University of North Dakota, Grand
    Forks

OHIO
Bowling Green State University-
    Bowling Green
John Carroll University
Kent State University, Kent
Miami University
Ohio University
University of Cincinnati
University of Toledo

OKLAHOMA
Oklahoma State University
Oral Roberts University
University of Tulsa

OREGON
Mt. Hood Community College
Oregon State University
Southern Oregon State College
University of Oregon

PENNSYLVANIA
Edinboro State College
Elizabethtown College
Kutztown State College
LaSalle College
Pennsylvania State University,
    University Park
Pennsylvania State University, Wilkes-
    Barre
Philadelphia College of Art
Seton Hill College

Temple University
California State College/Pennsylvania

PUERTO RICO
Inter-American University of Puerto
  Rico

SOUTH CAROLINA
Benedict College
Bob Jones University
University of South Carolina,
    Columbia

SOUTH DAKOTA
Black Hills State College
South Dakota State University

TENNESSEE
Middle Tennessee State University
Southern Missionary College
Southwestern at Memphis
University of Tennessee, Knoxville
University of Tennessee, Martin

TEXAS
Baylor University
Central Texas College
Corpus Christi State University
North Texas State University
Prairie View A&M University
Sam Houston State University
Southern Methodist University
Stephen F. Austin State University
Texas A&I University, Kingsville

Texas Southern University
Texas Woman's University
University of Houston, Houston
University of Texas at Austin
University of Texas at El Paso

UTAH
Brigham Young University
University of Utah
Weber State College

VERMONT
Castleton State College

VIRGINIA
Virginia Commonwealth University

WASHINGTON
Eastern Washington State College
Pacific Lutheran University
Western State University
Western Washington State College

WEST VIRGINIA
Marshall University

WISCONSIN
University of Wisconsin-La Crosse
University of Wisconsin-Madison
University of Wisconsin-Milwaukee
University of Wisconsin-Stevens Point
University of Wisconsin-Superior

GUAM
University of Guam

An Annotated Bibliography for the TV Writer

1. TV Series Presentations

Miller, Merle and Evan Rhodes. *Only You, Dick Daring.* New York: William Sloan and Associates, 1964. This remains a classic demonstration of how a pilot is developed by the writer, aborted by the studio, and mangled by the network.

Shanks, Bob. *The Cool Fire: How to Make it in Television.* New York: Vintage Books, 1977. This paperback is *essential* reading. Shanks offers unique and personal insights into the television industry from programming to production. He also has a very strong chapter on presentations and scripting.

Whitfield, Steve and Gene Roddenberry. *The Making of Star Trek.* New York: Ballantine Books, 1972. This paperback provides an excellent account of how the series was put together, from conception and development to sale and production. The original series presentation is included.

2. Grants & Non-Commercial Funding

Annual Register of Grant Support. Chicago: Marquis Academic Media. This annual register offers information on writing proposals and provides an index to grant programs catalogued by subject, *e.g.* media.

Brown, James W., ed. *Educational Media Yearbook.* New York: R. R. Bowker. This annual publication lists federal funding sources for new projects in television and film.

Catalog of Federal Domestic Assistance. Washington, D.C.: U.S. Government Printing Office. This is an annual compilation of all RFP's (requests for proposals).

Coe, Linda, ed. *Cultural Directory: A Guide to Federal Funds and Services for Cultural Activities.* New York: Associated Councils of the Arts. This directory identifies the federal funding programs available for individual artists and artistic organizations.

Film/Television: Grants, Scholarships, Special Programs. Washington, D.C.: The American Film Institute, National Education Services, Factfile series #12 grants and awards in film and television.

Gadney's Guide to 1800 International Contests, Festivals, & Grants in Film & Video. Glendale, Calif. Festival Publications. A cross-indexed reference for worldwide grants and competitive events in film, video, writing, and broadcasting.

Guide to College Courses in Film and Television. 6th ed., Washington, D.C.: The American Film Institute, National Education Series (1978). An excellent reference for scholarships, course offerings, and broadcast-film programs throughout the United States.

Guidelines and Formats for Submitting Program Production Proposals. Washington, D.C.: Corporation for Public Broadcasting. Guidelines established by CPB for submitting new program proposals.

Handbook for Independent Producers, Filmmakers, and Videomakers. New York: WNET-TV, Department of Program Planning. This brochure outlines the submission process for new projects at WNET-TV.

National Endowment for the Arts (NEA), Washington, D.C., publishes annual guidelines pertaining to their grant programs:
—*"Guide to Programs"* provides information about the Endowment's major program areas. Write to NEA, Program Information Office (Mail Stop 550) for a copy.
—*"Literature Program"* describes the support available for creative writers. Write to NEA, Literature Program (Mail Stop 607) for a copy of the guidelines.
—*"Media Arts: Film/Radio/Television"* describes the requirements for production aid and fellowships. Write to NEA, Media Arts Program (Mail Stop 552) for a copy of the guidelines.
—*"Theatre Program"* describes the support available to new playwrights and theatre companies. Write to NEA, Theatre Program (Mail Stop 554) for a copy of the guidelines.

National Endowment for the Humanities (NEH), Washington, D.C., publishes annual guidelines pertaining to their grant programs:
—*"Program Announcement"* provides information about the Endowment's major program areas. Write to NEH, Public Information Office for a copy.
—*"Media Humanities Projects"* describes the requirements for script development and production support. Write to NEH, Division of Public Programs (Mail Stop 403) for guidelines.

Mayer, Robert A. *What Will a Foundation Look for When You Submit a Grant Proposal?* New York: The Foundation Center, 1976. A very sound and useful guideline for writing grant proposals and seeking foundation support.

Milsaps, Daniel. *Grants and Aid to Individuals in the Arts,* 4th ed. Washington, D.C.: Washington International Arts Letter, 1978. This lists over a thousand foundations and agencies which support the arts (including TV and film programs).

Noe, Lee, ed. *The Foundation Grants Index.* New York: The Foundation Center. Annual. This catalogues the yearly grant activity of several hundred American foundations.

Orlich, Donald C. and Patricia Rend. *The Art of Writing Successful R&D Pro-*

posals. Pleasantville, N.Y.: Redgrave Publishing Company, 1976. A practical guide to writing research and development proposals.

Scholarships in Radio and Television. Washington, D.C.: National Association of Broadcasters, 1975. A listing of available opportunities for fellowships and scholarships in broadcasting.

White, Virginia P. *Grants: How to Find Out About Them and What to Do Next.* New York: Plenum Press, 1975. A very useful publication on grant writing and funding sources.

3. Periodicals on Grants

"A.F.I. Education Newsletter"
JFK Center for Performing Arts
Washington, D.C. 20506
> Bi-monthly newsletter lists new publications, grant announcements, and resources in film education.

"Arts Reporting Service"
9214 Three Oaks Drive
Silver Spring, MD 20910
> Bi-weekly newsletter on arts organizations and funding in the area.

"Communication Notes"
Council of Communication Societies
P.O. Box 1074
Silver Spring, MD 20910
> Monthly listing of events, awards, scholarships in communication.

"The Cultural Post"
National Endowment for the Arts (Mail Stop 550)
Washington, D.C. 20506
> Free bi-monthly newspaper that gives up-to-date information about grant activities in the arts.

"Foundation News"
Box 783
Old Chelsea Station
New York, NY 10011
> Bi-monthly index of grants awarded (in excess of $5,000). Published by Council on Foundations.

"The Grantsmanship Center News"
1015 West Olympic Blvd.
Los Angeles, CA 90015
> Bi-monthly newsletter on relevant issues, grant deadlines, new publications of interest.

"Ocular"
Ocular Publishing
1549 Platte St.
Denver, Col. 80202
> Quarterly publication on grant opportunities for artists, awards, and relevant issues.

"Washington International Arts Letter"
P.O. Box 9005
Washington, D.C. 20003

Monthly newsletter which covers the spectrum of politics, legislation, and grant opportunities for artists.

4. Dramatic Theory and Story Development

Archer, William. *Playmaking*. New York: Dodd, Mead & Co., 1912. Archer had no striking dramatic theory, but he sets out to *disprove* Bruntiere's law. He felt that crisis (rather than conflict of wills) is the chief requirement of drama. He was an early 20th century English critic.

Aristotle. *The Poetics*. (See S. H. Butcher.) Aristotle provided the first codification of dramatic theory in classic Greek times. He thought plot was the most important element in a play, and that it should be unified in time, place and action. He defined drama, partially, as an imitation of an action that is serious, complete, and of a certain magnitude. In his view, the impact of good drama creates an emotional catharsis for the audience.

Baker, George Pierce. *Dramatic Technique*. Boston: Houghton, Mifflin Co., 1919. Baker was the granddaddy of American playwriting teachers. He felt that a writer's major objective is to create an action which is capable of arousing audience emotions. The chief essential of drama is *action*.

Bentley, Eric. *Life of the Drama*. New York: Atheneum, 1964. This is a thought-provoking work by an outstanding contemporary American critic. Bentley parallels Aristotelian theory.

———.*The Playwright as Thinker: A Study of Drama in Modern Times*. New York: Harcourt, Brace, & World, rev. 1967. An excellent work of dramatic criticism, pointing to the problem of commercialism vs. art in theatre, and examining the work of selected playwrights.

Bruntiere, Ferdinand. *The Law of the Drama*. (1914). In Barrett H. Clark, *European Theories of the Drama*. Rev. ed. New York: D. Appleton-Century Co., 1965. Bruntiere was an important late 19th century French critic, extending Aristotle's concept of "conflict" in drama. Bruntiere proposed that drama is based on the conflict of wills among characters.

Butcher, S. H. *Aristotle's Theory of Poetry and Fine Art, With a Critical Text and Translation of the Poetics*. (Prefatory essay by John Gassner). New York: Dover Publications, 1951. This is one of the best translations of Aristotle's *Poetics*.

Clark, Barret H., ed. *European Theories of the Drama*. Rev. ed. New York: Crown Publishers, 1945; 1965. This is a classic resource for European dramatic theory.

Cole, Toby, ed. *Playwrights on Playwriting*. New York: Dramabook, 1961. An excellent compilation of theories, philosophies, and creative techniques expressed by a range of 20th century playwrights.

Dukore, Bernard, ed. *Dramatic Theory & Criticism: Greeks to Grotowski*. New York: Holt, Rinehart, & Winston, 1974. An excellent volume of dramatic criticism, excerpted from major writings of each period (classic times through late 20th century).

Egri, Lajos. *The Art of Dramatic Writing.* New York: Simon and Schuster, 1966. This is one of the most important and useful books for any writer of television, film, or the stage. Egri deals with the theory and technique of character development, premise construction, and building of conflict.

Olson, Elder. *Tragedy and Theory of Drama.* Detroit: Wayne State University Press, 1961. Olson agrees with Aristotle that plot governs character, but feels that any formal ordering of dramatic elements is too restrictive. Dramatic action is primarily interpersonal in Olson's point of view.

5. "The Method" and Character Development

Easty, Edward. *On Method Acting.* New York: House of Collectibles, Inc., 1966. This is a book that is used by actors trained in the Lee Strasberg Theatre Institute, where "The Method" is still being taught, in New York and Los Angeles.

Hethmon, Robert, ed. *Strasberg at the Actors Studio.* New York: The Viking Press Inc., 1965. This book is transcribed from tape recordings of Lee Strasberg teaching *The Method* at the Actor's Studio.

Lewis, Robert. *Method—or Madness.* New York: French & European Publications, Inc., 1958. A down-to-earth discussion of the Stanislavski system which was modified by Lee Strasberg at the Actor's Studio. *"The Method"* is defined, with strong points and weak points illuminated.

Magarshack, David. *Stanislavski on the Art of the Stage.* New York: Hill and Wang, 1961. Includes a collection of lectures by Stanislavski, "The System and Method of Creative Art." The introduction offers a simple and useful summary of Stanislavski's theory and techniques.

Moore, Sonia. *The Stanislavski System.* New York: The Viking Press, 1974. An easy-to-read handbook of Stanislavski's system of acting and character development.

Stanislavski, Constantin. *An Actor Prepares.* Trans. Elizabeth Reynolds Hapgood. New York: Theatre Arts Books, 1936. This book outlines the basic principles of finding inner truth, objectives, super-objectives, and through-lines of action.

———. *Building a Character.* Trans. Elizabeth Reynolds Hapgood. New York: Theatre Arts Books, 1949. This work concentrates on "outer technique" for the actor. Initially it was not as well known as the other two Stanislavski works.

———. *Creating a Role.* Trans. Elizabeth Reynolds Hapgood. New York: Theatre Arts Books, 1961. This book covers script analysis and character development techniques for the actor.

6. TV Writing Techniques

Brady, Ben. *The Keys to Writing for Television and Film,* Dubuque, Iowa: Kendall-Hunt, 3rd ed., 1978. Examines the dramatic structure of writing for TV and films, with script samples.

Coopersmith, Jerome. *Professional Writer's Teleplay/Screenplay Format.* New York: Writers Guild of America, East, 22 West 48th St., 1977. A very concise and informative booklet that provides detailed script models and formats. This is a *must* for the new TV writer.

Cousin, Michel. *Writing a Television Play.* Boston: Writer, Inc., 1975. A guide to visual and dramatic requirements in scripting.

Field, Stanley. *Professional Broadcast Writer's Handbook.* Blue Ridge Summit, Pa.: TAB books, 1974. A manual with samples.

Herman, Lewis. *A Practical Manual of Screen Playwriting.* Cleveland: World Publishing, 1963. Offers solid theory and practice of writing for motion pictures and TV films.

Hilliard, Robert L. *Writing for Television and Radio.* 3rd ed. New York: Hastings House, 1976. Presents concrete approaches to professional writing in all TV program formats and genres. In addition, each chapter is supplemented by practical exercises and suggested reference sources.

Lee, Robert and Robert Misiorowski. *Script Models: A Handbook for the Media Writer.* New York: Hastings House, 1978. Offers specific formats and script samples.

Swain, Dwight V. *Film Scriptwriting: A Practical Manual.* New York: Hastings House, 1976. This book deals with the basic techniques and tools of writing fact films (for clients) and feature films, with samples.

Trapnell, Coles. *Teleplay: An Introduction to Television Writing.* New York: Hawthorn Books, 1974. A basic introduction to form and technique.

Vale, Eugene. *Technique of Screenplay Writing.* New York: Grosset and Dunlap, 1972. A practical approach to scriptwriting, with samples.

Willis, Edgar E. *Writing TV and Radio Programs.* New York: Holt, Rinehart and Winston, 1967. An examination of dramatic and non-dramatic writing for TV & radio, with script samples.

Wylie, Max. *Writing for Television.* New York: Cowles Book Co., 1970. A professional look at form and structure, with script samples.

7. Marketing Resources

"Agencies That Have Subscribed to the Writers Guild of America—Artists Manager Basic Agreement." The list of agents includes those who will consider material from new writers. At no cost from the Writers Guild of America, West, 8955 Beverly Blvd., Los Angeles, Calif. 90048.

Bluem, A. William and Jason E. Squire, eds. *The Movie Business: American Film Industry Practice.* New York: Hastings House, 1973. A compilation of articles by professionals in the industry, including a section on story and screenplay.

Froug, William, ed. *The Screenwriter Looks at the Screenwriter.* New York: Dell Publishing, 1972. An unusually informative compilation of interviews with outspoken screenwriters, who discuss their theories and thoughts on writing as a profession.

"Schedule of Minimums, W.G.A. Theatrical and Television Basic Agreement." A summary of all the basic writing minimums. Contact the Writers Guild of America West, 8955 Beverly Blvd., Los Angeles, Calif. 90048.

Shanks, Bob. *The Cool Fire: How to Make it in Television.* New York: Vintage Books, 1977. One of the best books on the creative and executive spheres of television, including chapters on presentations and scripting.

Index